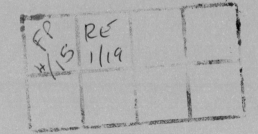

GREAT GARDEN DESIGN

GREAT GARDEN DESIGN

IAN HODGSON

F

FRANCES LINCOLN LIMITED
PUBLISHERS

Frances Lincoln Limited
74–77 White Lion Street
Islington N1 9PF
www.franceslincoln.com

Great Garden Design
Copyright © Frances Lincoln Limited 2015
Text copyright © Ian Hodgson 2015
Photographs copyright © see page 175
First Frances Lincoln edition 2015

Edited by Zia Allaway
Designed by Becky Clarke

CONTENTS

A catalogue record for this book is available from the
British Library

ISBN 978-0-7112-3573-1

Printed in China

9 8 7 6 5 4 3 2 1

Foreword
by John Brookes

Great Garden Design is a wholly refreshing book – in its presentation and in its content. The book breaks down the overall plan of a garden and deals with the various sections and functions it may include. I was particularly interested in the section 'Gardens with a Conscience', which outlines sustainable solutions, green technologies and the support of wildlife. This is indeed an interesting advance in garden thinking, and the author is to be commended for including it. This gentle introduction of modern technologies, showing how they can work even on a domestic scale is, I think, vital.

Indeed, this book covers a subject close to my heart. The Society of Garden Designers was founded in 1981 – when I was working abroad – not only to bring together the newly trained, as garden design courses of varying durations sprang up, but to also install a design criteria into our garden layouts. During that year, the Society's founders, Robin Williams, Rosemary Alexander, Peter Rogers and James Seymour, gathered together designers in order to establish an independent voice, and to collaborate effectively with the Royal Horticultural Society. This would ensure a professional presence at the world's most celebrated annual garden design competition, the RHS Chelsea Flower Show. As then, Chelsea is one of the few showcases for contemporary garden designs, and its trends, plants and styles are examined around the world, long after the one-week show closes.

However, the great majority of designers' projects are not show gardens, but real gardens that the designers conceive and make in collaboration with owners. Real-life gardens that need to evolve, delight and function for 52 weeks of the year, rather than a single week. Often these private spaces are unseen by the public, unless the owners choose to open them for the National Gardens Scheme or another charity, or allow them to be professionally photographed. Well, now you can see many of these real-life private gardens in all their glory within the pages of this book.

The influence of the founding SGD members cannot be underestimated. They have been involved in establishing design schools, offering employment, nurturing new designers, and producing television shows, books and journals. Garden design has advanced hugely and it is gratifying to see that many of the Society's members are exporting their talents. British garden designers have earned the reputation as some of the best in the world.

The Society has moved on in leaps and bounds, and this volume is a true reflection of the excellent work that its members are creating, worldwide. I wish both well.

John Brookes, MBE

A long-standing member of the Society of Garden Designers, John Brookes (right) is one of the most influential designers of recent times. His own garden, Denmans, in Sussex (below) was considered ground-breaking when he created it during the 1980s, and it is still admired today by fellow designers and visitors from around the world.

Introduction
by Ian Hodgson

GARDEN DESIGN galvanises art, science, culture and environment together unlike any other discipline. Gardens have been at the heart of human civilisation for thousands of years, but in the last few decades, their design has become more diverse, with new ideas fuelled particularly by concern for wildlife and the environment. A desire to improve our quality of life and reconnect with nature has also been an impetus for garden-making, from private courtyards to country estates and public spaces, but especially for recuperative gardens, where sensitive design of outdoor spaces can be a powerful agent for good.

This book identifies a range of ideas and themes that will help transform your outdoor space, using examples from members of the Society of Garden Designers. The first chapter 'Bold Visions, Great Designs' takes a look at particular styles, from contemporary formal and urban to cottage, country, naturalistic and meadow gardens, as well as themed subtropical and water gardens. The chapter also profiles designers that have produced some of the best examples of each genre.

The second chapter, 'Garden Gallery', is split into architectural ideas and planting styles, and here we take a closer look at all the elements and approaches used to create a garden, showcasing a range of inspirational features

This contemporary space shows how skilful design can transform a garden into a beautiful landscape, using just a small palette of plants and a creative eye for colour, shape and form.

DESIGN BY WILSON MCWILLIAM

and schemes. Design is, of course, a personal persuasion and all the examples presented can be reinterpreted and repurposed to create your garden, perhaps even founding your own unique style!

Gardens are also about having fun and enjoying life. 'Outdoor Experiences' illustrates this with the wide range of activities you can include in your design, from the purely passive to the highly active, including relaxing, dining, exercising and den-making. Environmental concerns form the basis of 'Gardens With A Conscience', which highlights some of the techniques designers use to make better use of natural resources, such as water, sunlight, and materials found on site or in the locality. These practices also help us tread more lightly on the earth, reducing our carbon footprint and allowing us to take greater responsibility for the demands we make on its resources. The realisation by scientists and environmentalists that gardens provide important refuges for a wide spectrum of wildlife is one of the great breakthroughs of the last decade. Their significance is set against a backdrop of dwindling natural habitats caused by intensive agriculture, urbanisation and climate change.

The final part of the book, 'Realising Your Design', provides practical advice on how to assess your site and commission a designer, with the directory of members of the Society of Garden Designers to help you make your choice. I hope the rich seam of creativity presented on these pages offers you a wealth of ideas and inspiration from the collective vision of these talented individuals.

BOLD VISIONS, GREAT DESIGNS

CONTEMPORARY GARDEN STYLES

GARDENS ARE EXCITING and dynamic places. They play with our emotions, positively influence our sense of wellbeing and connect us to the natural world, creating glorious alchemies of art and science that tap into the bedrock of our cultural existence.

Sourcing inspiration

What we personally want and need from gardens and how we interact with them are as multi-various as our personalities. Practicalities aside, personal history, culture, taste and vision all play a part in influencing our needs and aspirations for our outdoor spaces. We may yearn for something bold and uncompromising, minimalist and highly architectural, wild and romantic, or just simply a refuge from the worries of the world. Often, the difficulty is pinning down that vision or idea and making it a practical reality. Conversely, you may not know what you want and seek inspiration, perhaps assembling a portfolio of ideas from books, photographs, magazine articles or the internet. In either case, you can start by considering a range of garden design styles, as shown on the pages of this chapter, to find a look that suits you best. You can then evolve it to create a design of your own or commission an experienced garden designer, such as one of the professionals who belong to the Society of Garden Designers (SGD).

Choosing a style

While there is nothing to stop you choosing any style you wish or taking a completely personal approach, some

LEFT The interplay of shapes and forms sets up a dynamic rhythm across a series of shallow terraces, while the linear timber walkway effortlessly spirits the eye and body across the landscape into the space beyond.

DESIGN BY TOM STUART-SMITH

ABOVE Repeated drifts of ornamental perennials coalesce to mimic the structure of natural plant communities. Although the effect looks random, plants are carefully blended to provide year-round interest.

DESIGN BY DAN PEARSON

ABOVE The artful and potent use of lighting can transform a garden space into a theatrical stage set at night, either to be viewed remotely from indoors or to immerse yourself in while hosting a social event outside.

DESIGN BY ANDREW FISHER TOMLIN

BELOW Selecting an item of furniture is just as critical as choosing a piece of sculpture when establishing the theme or style of a garden, as its design and colour exert a powerful influence on the overall look.

DESIGN BY CHARLOTTE ROWE

designs and the dynamics that underpin them may be more appropriate to your situation than others. Sensitivity to sense of place, historical nuances and the intrinsic elements that determine the character or use of the space can provide inspiration and guide the direction of your design. Formal gardens, either period or contemporary, are often attractive propositions as they are relatively easy to create, using strong geometrical forms and a restricted palette of materials. While they do provide opportunities for dramatic theatre, their geometry and the scale and proportion of the various elements should be your primary consideration when evolving this style.

Cottage, country and naturalistic gardens involve the creative use of plants and, while rewarding, they are demanding in terms of the time, skills and effort required to manage them effectively. The same is true for a tropical-style garden, which would suit an enthusiastic plant lover. The species and varieties you choose are critical to the success of these styles, although structural planting is essential, providing the bones of the garden. Plants with varying seasons of interest are crucial, too, helping to carry the style throughout the year, and foliage is more valuable than flowers, so get to know a range of plants with colourful or dramatic leaves. Also ensure your plant selections are appropriate to the space; varieties that are ideal for expansive landscapes may be inappropriate for small gardens.

Water is probably the most dynamic element you can include in your garden. Essential to our own wellbeing, water also sustains wildlife and helps to increase biodiversity, so before creating a feature, decide if it will be for you, wildlife, or both, as this will determine the design and the way it is managed.

Maintaining the look

One of the most important considerations when designing a garden is how you will maintain it. No garden is completely maintenance free: plants are living things and require regular care, such as mowing, pruning, training, feeding and watering, to maintain their appearance and long-term performance. You may be a willing participant, relishing the opportunity to nurture and develop your garden, or, equally, you may want to delegate the responsibility to someone else. Either way, it is an aspect you will need to consider from the outset, and if planning to use a gardener to help with maintenance, ensure that this cost is factored into your thinking.

The following chapter showcases the work of a range of leading designers and design styles, providing you with a rich seam of inspiration and illustrating what can be achieved in gardens of all shapes and sizes.

BELOW Realised through the use of different features and materials, the powerful lines in this design create a dramatic picture, with the clean shapes of the architecture contrasting with woodland plants and box spheres.

DESIGN BY SARA JANE ROTHWELL

RIGHT Textured treatments of the boundary provide interest in this minimalist-style room outdoors. A log fire inset into an imposing chimney breast adds a practical feature while maintaining the design intention.

DESIGN BY DEAKINLOCK

The alignment of geometric shapes
fuses architectural elements with tightly
trained plant forms to create a tranquil,
but carefully controlled space. Use of high
calibre materials underpins the style.

DESIGN BY DEL BUONO GAZERWITZ

Contemporary formal

CRISP AND CLEAN, formal gardens' distinctive style combines strict symmetry, geometric shapes and structural plant forms. Ideal for both urban and country settings, these designs are perfect for those who like a sense of order and are prepared to invest in good quality materials to create the look.

Geometric principles

Of all the various styles, the formal garden is the one most readily identified and perhaps the most imposing. The use of strong lines and geometry to create a hierarchy of interrelated and interlocking shapes exerts a powerful effect on the landscape, one brimming with confidence and self-assertion, and seemingly offering the opportunity for tight control and ascendancy over nature. Results are crisp and clean-cut, with blocks, rectangles and other geometric shapes realised in hard and soft landscaping materials, while the interplay of scale, proportion and perspective generates a wealth of drama and theatrical effects.

Formal designs can be employed with great success in almost any space, large or small. They can be used to recreate an ornate period piece or to produce something radical and contemporary, or austere and minimalist. If you have never designed before, the formal style is also one of the simplest to employ, as shapes are rigidly geometric and easily linked together to produce an aesthetically pleasing picture.

Symmetry is central to the design of a traditional formal garden, with features mirrored on either side of a central axis, often a path or lawn. Motifs, in terms of designed spaces or elements, such as patterns in paving or topiary spheres, are often repeated either side of the axis to provide visual harmony, or slightly askew to strike a note of discord. Designers of formal style also link the garden to the house or other buildings by aligning key elements, such as paths, terraces and lawns, with the windows, doors or gateways, thereby extending the architecture into the landscape. The ground plan of the garden may also closely reflect the floor spaces within the house. In traditional large formal gardens, this alignment becomes looser and more informal with distance from the building, before merging into the surrounding landscape, but because the space around most homes today is at a premium, this is not always possible or practicable.

Many gardens include formal elements, whether it is the geometric shape of borders, alignment of a straight pathway or arrangement of vistas, but these are often subsequently blurred by other features that are more casually positioned. It is only when geometrical elements and their mathematical arrangement predominate that the powerful effect of the truly formal garden is realised.

Roots in history

Formal design has its roots in the 17th century gardens of the great French and particularly the Italian palaces. Designers of today have been influenced by the famous terrace gardens cut into the mountainous northern Italian

KNOTS AND PARTERRES

Intricate arrangements of low growing evergreen foliage plants, knot gardens are designed to give the impression of interlocking lengths of rope, giving rise to the name, and are especially effective when viewed from an elevated position, such as an upstairs window. They were introduced to Britain during the reign of Elizabeth I, and influenced by the garden designs of Italy. Most were highly symbolic, depicting messages of love, the family crest or elements found in the house; others were simply puzzles to be solved. Historically, cotton lavender (*Santolina*), thrift (*Armeria maritima*) and myrtle (*Myrtus communis*) were used to create the knots, with box (*Buxus sempervirens*) becoming popular later. In Tudor times the gaps between the structural plants were filled with crushed brick, sands, or even coal, but today designers have a wealth of colourful gravels and materials to choose from. Alternatively, you can fill the gaps with spring bulbs and summer bedding or colourful ground-cover plants to create seasonal interest.

Parterre gardens are similar to knots, but the structural plants are not designed to overlap like rope. Examples of traditional parterres can be seen in the formal Renaissance gardens of Europe, such as those at Villandry in France, where clipped box is laid out in intricate patterns. Today, designers often use simpler geometric shapes to produce similar effects.

A formal parterre garden design by Nigel Philips

landscape, such as the Villa d'Este and the Boboli gardens, as well as the formal parterre gardens, including Versailles and Vaux le Vicomte in the Loire Valley in France.

Contemporary designs also make reference to design principles developed by ancient cultures, such as those of Greece, Persia and Rome, which featured cloistered or open courtyard gardens that offered shade, shelter and repose from the dry, sun-beaten climate. These oases included still water, fountains and trees to promote reflection and quiet contemplation, with flowers to stimulate the senses.

Modern developments

Contemporary designers of formal gardens often combine the classical principles seen in these historic gardens with a more minimalist approach, and may also include elements of Modernist style in their work.

Modernism in garden design takes its influence from a number of 20th century artistic and cultural movements, from Cubism and the Bauhaus school to the work of Dutch artist Piet Mondrian, as well as influential architects, such as Le Corbusier, Frank Lloyd Wright and Luis Barragán. Like formal style, use of strong geometry underpins the approach, but designs tend to be asymmetrical, while the philosophy that 'form follows function' is often used to shape and characterise the space. Recent developments in technology also inform designs, with structures made from modern materials, including concrete, glass, plastic and metal. Planar surfaces of different textures are frequently aligned or intersected in stark, yet serene contrast, while architectural frameworks for buildings and walls are sometimes left exposed, demonstrating their functionality.

Designers select paving materials, such as polished or finely sawn stone, for their sublime surface properties, and they may also use expanses of fine gravel to lend subtle colour and texture. Closely mown turf, when included, provides a soothing foil for the hard landscape and planting.

Bright colour is employed sparingly and potently in these designs, perhaps in the furniture or on a wall, and the interplay of light and shade helps to generate atmosphere. The designer's aim is to bring together all the elements in understated layers to build a framework, while abstract

works of art or sculpture, together with water, often dramatically illuminated, provide powerful focal points.

Contemporary formal planting designs

Structural plant forms are used sparingly in both formal and Modernist-inspired gardens. Crisply clipped hedges of yew, box or deciduous hornbeam provide barriers, edges or blocks to reinforce the design. Pleached hornbeam or lime, with branches trained to create elevated screens of

LEFT An elevated geometrical canopy pierced by a cluster of copper rods creates a striking tableau. The contemporary style contrasts with the ancient technique used to build the rammed earth walling.

DESIGN BY WILSON MCWILLIAM

BELOW Symmetrical blocks of yew anchor quartets of golden Catalpa around a central rill, which commands the vista back to the house. The unfettered clarity of the central design maintains the sense of formality.

DESIGN BY PAUL BAINES

foliage atop bare trunks, are also used to provide privacy and control views through the space. Topiary is popular in contemporary formal designs, with pyramids, cubes, globes or cylinders carved from bay, box, holly, yew or Portuguese laurel. Spaces may also be punctuated with trees and large shrubs pruned to raise their canopies to expose decorative stems, or with cloud-pruned specimens planted at strategic points or in large, elegant containers. Cloud pruning, a style that originated in China and Japan, crafts multi-stemmed specimens of fine-leaved shrubs, such as *Ilex crenata*, into elevated globes of foliage to produce striking features. Flowering plants, if used, are confined to particular beds, which may be filled with colour-themed seasonal bedding, monochromatic flowers and foliage, or naturalistic-style plantings to counterpoint the formality.

Decorative highlights

Even though the current trend is for quiet, contemplative spaces that utilise a restrained palette of colours, contemporary and formal gardens can be made vibrant through the use of paving, gravel and artifacts, or with splashes of brightly coloured foliage and flower. The trick is to weave together colourful elements so they do not overwhelm each other to maintain the elegant look.

BELOW A selection of clipped and statuesque plant forms, including hornbeam hedges and upright and globular yew specimens, punctuate these interconnected spaces.

DESIGN BY TOM STUART-SMITH

RIGHT A paved courtyard populated by clipped box hedges, artfully used to outline the various beds, lends a sense of formality and helps to guide the eye through the open spaces.

DESIGN BY ANDY STURGEON

Designers often include sculptures or artworks to decorate formal designs, providing incidental interest or a dramatic focus for a vista, their impact intensified by the absence of floral distraction. Contemporary works of art with simple, clean lines in polished stone or metal, blend perfectly into a formal design, while elevated stone friezes make dramatic focal points where ground space is at a premium. Static or moving water can enliven a space, too, a single fountain, cascade or film conveying movement, reflection and sound.

As furniture is the main functional item in the garden and on permanent display, it should be chosen with care and embody or complement the nature of the design in some way, through shape, texture or colour. Painting mismatched structures, such as timber chairs and tables, in a single understated tone throughout will help provide visual cohesion, with restrained flourishes of gilt paint enhancing the theatricality of the design.

ABOVE Complementary dark-toned surfaces inset with repeated plant motifs are the ying and yang of this Modernist-inspired town garden, with planting neatly confined to the margins.

DESIGN BY CHARLOTTE ROWE

Dramatic sculpture

The serene setting framing this iconic sculpture make it a powerful focal point. Water and lighting below enliven the scene both day and night.

Formal hedging

Tiered hedging both reinforces the geometry of the space and leads the eye into the garden. The hedge surfaces also reflect light.

Restful lawn

By acting as a foil, the expanse of neatly manicured turf prepares the eye for the drama ahead. Black tile edging boldly frames the space, while also acting as a mowing strip.

Perfect patio

Crisp, cream-toned stone imparts a restful, high-calibre finish to the patio, and a visual link to the sculpture beyond.

CASE STUDY

DESIGN BY LUCIANO GIUBBILEI

A contemporary formal garden

This tree-shrouded garden is located behind a Victorian house in central London, and the aim was to realise an outdoor space that complemented the proportions of the rooms within, with a stone-clad patio of identical tone to the flooring inside. Layered greenery and trees play a crucial role in creating the quiet, contemplative atmosphere of the 25m x 20m (82ft x 66ft) space. The focal point is a bronze sculpture, 'Double Ellipse' by Nigel Hall RA, elegantly showcased on smooth rendered walls, its shadows playing across the surface. A shallow water feature by Andrew Ewing reflects the sculpture during daylight, while illuminated jets sparkle at night. Tiered hedges in box (*Buxus sempervirens*), yew (*Taxus baccata*), and Portugese laurel, (*Prunus lusitanica*), counterpoint the installation, and a cloak of Virginia creeper (*Parthenocissus*) provides potent autumnal colour. The whole edifice is set around a verdant lawn framed by charcoal basalt paviors.

LUCIANO GIUBBILEI

Italian-born Luciano studied at the Inchbald School of Design in London and set up his own practice in 1997. His philosophy embodies the arrangement of space and proportion of elements, including plants, materials and art, to create harmony, elegance and a sense of timelessness. He has won many awards, including gold medals at the RHS Chelsea Flower Show, as well as 'Best in Show' in 2014. Based in London, he is currently working on landscape projects in the UK, Europe and the USA.

Urban chic

STYLISH GARDENS in towns and cities fuse high quality materials with contemporary furnishings to create cool oases in the heart of the urban jungle. Large leafy plants rub shoulders with seasonal flowers in colour-coordinated schemes that complement the interior décor of the owner's home.

Clear visions

Small outdoor spaces designed and furnished to the highest specifications have come to define this approach to garden-making, but unlike many other styles, which have developed from an historic precedent that determines the design principles and stylistic execution, the urban garden is more a response to increasing population densities and shrinking outdoor spaces in our towns and cities.

Gardens can form part of an historic or period property, new-build housing development, apartment with a balcony or roofscape, or a shared community space, with each location influencing how they are designed and the features they accommodate. Many urban designs are an extension of the home; outdoor rooms visualised as spaces for indulging and enjoying a particular lifestyle, such as alfresco entertaining or relaxing. They also reflect the taste, needs, and personality of the owner or client and represent their cultural expectations and persuasions, making a statement about who they are and what they stand for. The garden may, for example, encompass a particular passion, such as an outdoor kitchen or a music or artist's studio.

Designs are interpreted in a wholly contemporary way with clarity and a simplicity of intent, underpinned by architectural styling and clean flowing lines that allow the built form and constructional materials to predominate and reinforce the look. Spaces are usually paved with high calibre materials, including granite, marble, or ashlar blocks in the most prestigious venues, or natural sandstone and hardwood decking in gardens where budgets are more limited.

Design considerations

The need for privacy and seclusion is an important design consideration in town gardens, with wall treatments such as trelliswork or pleached hedges raising the height of boundaries, while abiding by the legal limits that often apply in built-up areas. Designers may also need to find solutions to environmental factors that affect urban plots. For example, gardens can be awkwardly shaped and shaded by buildings, and spaces between densely packed housing often creates wind funnelling. However, these issues can usually be resolved with careful planning and strategic positioning of seating areas and screening. Changes of level, leading to basements or first-floor rooms, can be integrated into a design with verandahs and raised or sunken terraces that offer different views of the garden, turning problems into virtues.

Some outdoor spaces are so small and restricted that designers envision the garden as a piece of set design to be viewed from a conservatory or glass-fronted room, with high quality landscaping and planting providing a captivating panorama. Green wall technology also enables vertical

Cool green planting underpinned by crisp, formal design, pale stone paving and dark, mysterious water combines to create the tranquil ambience of this small enclosed city garden.

DESIGN BY CHARLOTTE ROWE

THE URBAN FRONT GARDEN

A sensitively designed front garden or entranceway can be just as chic as a rear garden. Designs have the potential to make an imposing and stylish statement to complement or appropriately contrast with the period style and façade of the property, perhaps also referencing the design at the back. Car parking can be integrated into the scheme, too, with a driveway or hardstanding that offers room for manoeuvring woven into a design that is both practical and attractive.

While paving over a front garden is considered unenvironmental because rainwater run-off collectively contributes to flash flooding, sand-jointed bricks or blocks, gravel, or one of the custom-made permeable products for driveways, offer good alternatives. Ground-cover planting, easy-care shrubs and seasonal flowers will help soften the landscape, with crevice plants, such as thyme, filling gaps between paving in areas where there is no car traffic. If considering parking the car off-road, check local legal regulations and the procedure for installing a drop kerb to enable entry.

Easy-care planting combines with a permeable gravel surface in a front garden by Cherry Mills

ABOVE LEFT The clean design of this functional space presents various options for alfresco dining whatever the weather: under cover, shaded beneath a vine-covered pergola, or basking in full sun.

DESIGN BY STUART CRAINE

ABOVE RIGHT This rendered wall, inset with alcoves, creates a tangible sense of the room outdoors, while complementary furniture and cushions add to the homely feel of the composition.

DESIGN BY MANDY BUCKLAND

surfaces to be softened and covered in a tapestry of foliage and flowers, and they help to insulate buildings. Green walls are not easy to perfect and you may need professional advice to ensure their longevity and effectiveness.

Planting plans

Planting in urban designs tends to be minimalist in style and subservient to the architecture. Evergreen climbers are often used to clothe walls and plants are set around the periphery or marshalled into raised beds to blur the hard lines of the landscaping. Evergreen shrubs and trees add permanent structure, while herbaceous perennials and bulbs provide seasonal highlights. Specimen plants, such as multi-stemmed trees and large shrubs, often with their crowns raised, are carefully chosen for their distinctive characteristics to act as focal points. Maples, white-stemmed birches and the June berry, *Amelanchier*, are popular choices. Trees are usually purchased as established specimens to provide an immediate sense of maturity; large plants can be craned into sites where access is restricted by the specialist nurseries or contractors that provide them.

Decorating the space

There are a number of key elements that have come to characterise urban gardens. Inspiration for decorating the space may derive from historical precedents, perhaps resonating with elements of the house façade or the cultural background of the owner. More frequently, however, designs will feature modern or retro-styled sculpture or a frieze, usually recherché and understated to reflect the style of the architecture.

Water is a popular design feature in many urban gardens, either acting as a focal point or an incidental element. Again, the approach is architectural in style, with water contained in geometric forms rather than natural-looking pools. Water surfaces may be still and reflective, animated with films of water running over metal or stone surfaces, or agitated to create rippling effects and soothing sounds. Where more drama and excitement is intended, designers often include blades of water falling from a chute. All of these features are easily designed into small gardens and take up very little space.

Lighting the garden so it can be enjoyed at night is another critical consideration. Lighting schemes are best designed and built into your garden at the outset, to make use of all the opportunities available. Its use for safety and security not withstanding, creative lighting designs, whether subtle or dramatic, can completely transform a small space at night. Ideas include integrating lights into planters and seating at ground level so that the features seem to float, and illuminating blades of water, translating them into moving sculpture. Modern digital technology, outdoor plasma screens and other innovations offer further scope for dramatic creative displays.

Tables, seating, and containers should visually integrate with the design in both colour and style, with soft furnishings, such as colourful cushions or throws, creating flamboyant flourishes. Pressure of space may mean that you cannot include all the decorative elements or features you desire, so prioritise your needs and what is important to you aesthetically. The secret is to keep the styling simple so that your design looks uncluttered and effortless.

LEFT Dramatic illumination of the water and landscaping transforms a feature that's chic by day into a powerful statement at night.

DESIGN BY JANINE PATTISON

Creating roof gardens

With urban green and garden space always at a premium, burgeoning interest and enthusiasm for roof gardens looks set to remain an aspiration for town and city dwellers, as well as urban planners. Technological advances mean that social spaces and gardens can be more easily created on any elevated locality, from balconies through to extensive shared and public amenities.

Some garden and landscape designers specialise in the creation of these facilities and can deliver sophisticated solutions to overcome a wide range of challenges. Theoretically, any style of garden can be created, from minimalist and urban chic designs through to wildlife gardens and leafy jungles, with moving water and creative lighting adding to the imaginative possibilities. However, minimalist designs are logistically the easiest to create, as the containers and soil needed to support large numbers of plants can be heavy and may not be possible on roofs with low load-bearing capacities.

Planting needs to be chosen with care to ensure it will tolerate the strong sunlight and high winds on a roof, especially when plants are young and growth is most vulnerable. Specialist composts for roof gardens are now available, which are light in weight and contain sufficient nutrients and minerals to support even large shrubs and trees. For large schemes, plan in advance a suitable irrigation system that will help to guarantee the sustainability of the planting in the long term.

The wide range of green wall and roof growing systems available will help you transform your outdoor space. You can choose a simple scheme, composed of elements to make the space comfortable for entertaining or relaxing, with plants in pots providing interest and helping to create screening for privacy and wind protection. 'Off-the-peg' products, such as lightweight, aluminium-framed furniture and fibreglass planters, are ideal for these owner-generated schemes, but if you desire something more sophisticated, adventurous and permanent, secure the services of an experienced designer, as there are a whole host of issues to consider, not least the minefield of legal and planning issues inherent in most roof garden projects.

Weighty issues

Whether you are creating the garden yourself or employing a designer, check building regulations and ask the planning authority if there are any restrictions before embarking on any project. Also employ a qualified civil engineer to assess the suitability of the space for a garden or ensure that your designer does so. The load-bearing capacity will need careful assessment to check that the weight of paving, architectural structures and planting is within limits. Drainage systems and the installation of a water supply to feed plant irrigation systems also need to be addressed at the design stage. The safety of users is another prime consideration, with properly installed barriers needed to secure the development. Pots and planters can pose a danger if they are toppled in high winds, and they should be fixed to the floor to prevent injury or damage to property.

FAR LEFT, TOP The primeval ambience of an open fire complements the substantial cubed timber seats that form the centrepiece of this roof terrace.

FAR LEFT, BOTTOM The dining area on this roof garden makes the most use of the restricted space, with a built-in bench and slim, elegant contemporary table and chairs.

LEFT Toughened glass safety barriers on this coastal roof garden protect it from prevailing winds, while providing clear views of the panorama beyond.

BELOW This elegant design takes into account the need for shade on a roof, using a sail and slatted fencing to shield the lounge area and trees that cast dappled light over the whole garden.

Shade-tolerant planting

Mature specimen of the wedding cake tree, *Cornus controversa*, with shrubby *Nandina domestica*, *Libertia*, ferns and hardy geraniums.

Planted paving

Arcs of block paving interplanted with mat-forming baby's tears, *Soleirolia soleirolii*, which can be walked on, create a curved transition between the house and main garden.

Serpentine wall and seating

The smooth, rendered wall with stone coping affords privacy, but allows views over and between to planting and lighting behind.

Raised boundary

A sunny wall is raised using a slatted timber screen for privacy, while the evergreen climber, *Trachelospermum*, softens the brickwork with a leafy screen.

Artistic influences

Yellow ochre rendering on the raised bed walls and off-white York and Portland stone paving reference artist Vermeer's colour palette.

CASE STUDY

DESIGN BY ANDY STURGEON

An urban garden

The design brief for this garden behind a Grade 1 listed property in London was that 'it should be like a Vermeer painting'. It had to also provide space for entertaining and be shielded from the windows of the terraced houses that overlook it. The designer was also keen to avoid a symmetrical, formal design, which is so often used when a nod to the past is called for. A 1.5m (5ft)-high sectional serpentine wall provides privacy when sitting in the garden, while also offering views over the top and through the gaps into the space behind, which features lighting and shade-tolerant plants. The integral bench is sculptural, yet accommodating, reducing the need for lots of free-standing furniture, and the palette of warm browns, pastel blues and off-white, in both the planting and hard materials, echo the work of the Dutch artist. Use of Portland and York stone help create the period ambience, and were also acceptable to the heritage authority involved in the project.

ANDY STURGEON

Acknowledged as one of the top ten designers in the UK by the Sunday Times and House and Garden Magazine, Andy Sturgeon has achieved six gold medals at the RHS Chelsea Flower Show, including Best in Show in 2010, as well as a number of other professional awards. A versatile designer, his commissions range from small roof terraces in urban areas to the gardens of large country estates, with projects in the UK, Europe, Japan and other parts of Asia. His design practice is based in Brighton.

Cottage and country style

CONFECTIONS OF FLOWERS, cottage and country gardens provide romantic settings for plant lovers. Cottage style is perfect for small plots, fusing beds of flowers, fruit and vegetables, while large gardens in the country offer space to accommodate a rich palette of shrubs, trees, perennials and bulbs.

The English tradition

If there are two styles that epitomise the essence of English tradition, they are cottage and country gardens. Although each is different in design and execution, both can be found in various permutations in gardens large and small throughout Britain. The styles also have a following worldwide and beautiful examples can be found in gardens from Japan to the United States.

Characterized by their focus on plants, the ebullience of flower and foliage is generated by all forms, from annuals, perennials and bulbs through to shrubs, trees and climbers. The balance of plant size and shape, their subsequent arrangement and the way they are managed delivers the styles' individuality, and reflects the spirit and ambience of approach. Herbaceous perennials, which are essentially plants that die down in winter, underpin both styles and provide the main floral interest from spring to autumn. They are also the components for that quintessential English invention, the 'herbaceous border'.

Cottage gardens

The cottage garden was born out of a stark necessity to grow food for those who worked on the land or lived in remote countryside communities. So the forerunners of the floral feast we see today were largely vegetable and fruit gardens, with perhaps a few favourite herbs and flowers included for cutting. 'Florists' flowers', which are plants that were collected, grown and developed by ordinary working people, also became key elements of the design style in the early 19th century. Some, including pinks (*Dianthus*) and auriculas (*Primula auricula*), had been in cultivation for hundreds of years, but easily grown introductions, such as dahlias and chrysanthemums, were quickly embraced and added to the repertoire. A romanticised version of the cottage garden started to evolve in the latter half of the 19th century, fuelled by the social and artistic movements of the day and influenced by Victorian authors like Shirley Hibberd and William Robinson, who promoted a more natural style of planting. Swathes of new plants, brought to Britain by bands of enthusiastic plant hunters, became available to the public for the first time and were adopted by devotees to the cottage style.

Translating the style

The cottage garden remains as popular today as it was 100 years ago, but its high maintenance requirements have limitations. As such, it is a good solution for smaller, domestic spaces, where the intricacy of plant combinations is better appreciated and tending them is easier to manage. However, with careful plant selection and more robust

A small paved terrace enveloped by lush
herbaceous and shrubby plants in pastel tones,
with old-fashioned roses providing structure,
epitomises romantic cottage and country styles.

DESIGN BY DAVID STEVENS

groupings, larger schemes are perfectly possible and maintenance can be minimised.

The cottage garden planting style is one of seemingly relaxed abandon, where annuals and perennials are allowed to mingle freely, shot through with seasonal effects from bulbs, such as snowdrops, tulips and daffodils. Staple vegetables and fruit trees also find a place in these designs, with small flowering trees, such as lilac and laburnum, and shrubs, including old-fashioned roses and hydrangeas, providing a structural backbone. Swags of honeysuckle, roses and clematis are used to festoon windows and doorways. Plants are also allowed to naturalise in gravel or other aggregates, adding to the naturalistic look of the garden. Contemporary designers of cottage garden style often colour theme plantings, frequently in pastel shades, to create romantic, dream-like effects, or they may blend the flowers with ornamental grasses, blurring the line between cottage and naturalistic designs.

The flower beds in these designs are usually intersected with informal pathways made from turf, gravel, bark chips or rustic paving, such as old brick or reclaimed paving slabs.

Country abundance

The country garden is an iconic British style, which still finds a place in modern gardens, having been reinvented in countless ways over time. As the name suggests, the style

LEFT Colourful flowers and textured foliage flood an intimate terrace, the focus of which is the imposing pastel-coloured period-style furniture. Box topiary adds a formal architectural note among the melee of plants.

DESIGN BY DAVID STEVENS

BELOW, LEFT Eye-catching tulips throng these spring borders, tonally complementing the flowering shrubs. Self-seeding perennials, such as aquilegias, primulas and foxgloves, could also be included into the scheme.

DESIGN BY CHARLES RUTHERFOORD

BELOW, RIGHT Relaxed naturalistic-style planting adds the right stylistic note to this open, sunny garden in the country. Rusty-coloured foxgloves, white echinacea, purple sedums and ornamental alliums provide the mainstay of this summer display.

DESIGN BY THOMAS HOBLYN

INSPIRING HERBACEOUS BORDERS

Decorative plantings of herbaceous plants have long been a feature of British gardens. In the 18th century, desirable perennial plants were collected together in the borders of country cottages, and these informal flower gardens were at the time acclaimed as a revolution in taste and sentiment. In 1844 the first double formal herbaceous borders were created at Arley Hall, near Manchester, which can still be seen today, but it was the creative influence of the Arts and Crafts movement in the late 19th and early 20th centuries that popularized their development and secured their future as staple elements of garden design. Notable examples are at Parham House in Sussex and Newby Hall in Ripon, North Yorkshire, acknowledged to be the longest in Europe.

Colour-themed plantings, such as the red borders at Hidcote in Gloucestershire, or progressions of colour, as seen at Killerton in Devon, also became popular in the 20th century. The 'mixed border', where shrubs are included to add structure, provide height and prolong the season of interest, developed as a way of alleviating the bare earth in winter, and many 21st century designers use this technique in modern settings, finding their inspiration from classic examples, such as the famous Long Border at Great Dixter in East Sussex.

Tom Stuart-Smith's borders at his own garden in Hertfordshire

developed to decorate the country seats of landowners and gentry, who had hitherto embraced the formal parterre gardens of the 17th and 18th centuries. A change in philosophy, driven by the Picturesque Movement in the mid to late 18th century, encouraged more natural planting designs, which were married to formal frameworks to create this lush, romantic style. The landscape was also decorated with recreational buildings, such as follies, statuary and decorative artifacts, while the planting, like that of cottage gardens, was influenced by late Pre-Raphaelite acolytes, such William Robinson, who advocated wild and naturalistic use of plants. The style was further embellished by the Arts and Crafts movement of the late 19th century and early 20th century, with the intricately woven, colour-themed plant groupings of Gertrude Jekyll, brought to life in the settings of Edwin Lutyens' timeless architecture and use of natural materials. Examples can be seen at Hestercombe in Somerset and Jekyll's own house at Munstead Wood in Surrey.

Contemporary interpretations

The modern country garden comprises an amalgam of elements. The garden may be divided with clipped hedges or walls into smaller compartments or 'outdoor rooms' close to the house, and planting designs are often themed or offer a range of visual experiences, such as single or double borders and water features. Geometric topiary or clipped and trained trees are used to punctuate the spaces, and statuary and seating, frequently made from rustic or local materials, provide focal points to complete vistas.

Architectural features, such as rose-clad pergolas and arbours, add drama and scale to the enterprise. Closely mown lawns provide the setting for these features and the planting, with gravel, brick or stone paviors used in highly trafficked areas. In larger gardens, the design is usually looser further from the house, with trees and shrubs, and naturalized bulbs and wild flowers set in grassland, and mown paths leading to secret or romantic refuges. Borrowed scenery and views to the countryside beyond may also form a part of the design, influencing the arrangement of the various elements and orientation of the design.

Structural hedging

Clipped yew hedges enclose the garden and create a visual foil for the plantings; yew buttresses subdivide the expansive borders.

Formal pleaching

An avenue of pleached lime trees and a yew hedge truncate the vista through the blue borders, while white alliums and variegated *Miscanthus* grasses catch the eye.

Box cones

Eye-catching focal points and preludes to the planting beyond, this quartet of box cones anchor the scheme into the landscape.

Herbaceous borders

Perennials are woven in asymmetric drifts, with tall *Delphinium* and *Eupatorium* at the back, fronted by *Nepeta*, *Achillea* and geraniums.

Creative paving

Cobbles in various sizes and tones were used to create this intricately patterned decoration. Cobbles can be inserted in situ or made into preformed units.

CASE STUDY

DESIGN BY ARABELLA LENNOX-BOYD

A country garden

The centrepiece of Arabella's 30-year old garden at Gresgarth Manor is a series of colour-themed gardens, including the 'Blue Border' (left), comprising a mix of blue, mauve and pink-flowered perennials, interspersed with foliage plants. The beds, which run east-west, are 22m (72ft) long and 4.5m (15ft) deep, allowing generous plantings to create sumptuous effects. Drifts are repeated across the borders in a rhythmic, but not symmetrical, way to avoid predictable formality, and enveloped by yew hedges with intermediate buttresses subtly subdividing the spaces. Careful planning lies behind a succession of seasonal interest. Spring bulbs fill gaps until the plantings swell in summer, while spent stems and seedheads provide winter interest. An intricate cobbled pathway by artist Maggie Howarth surrounds four box cones, and an avenue of pleached limes truncates the view at the end.

ARABELLA LENNOX-BOYD

One of the UK's leading landscape designers, Italian-born Arabella has created more than 400 gardens worldwide during her illustrious 40-year career, including six RHS Chelsea Flower Show gold medal-winnng exhibits. She also won Best in Show in 1998. She has served as a trustee of Kew Gardens, a member of The Historic Parks and Gardens Panel of English Heritage and was awarded the RHS Veitch medal for her outstanding contribution to horticulture. Her practice is in central London.

Ornamental grasses, such as Miscanthus,
Panicum and Stipa, are key elements of
naturalistic planting styles, the yellow
daisies of Rudbeckia, pink Echinacea and
gold Achillea enlivening summer designs.

DESIGN BY TOM STUART-SMITH

Naturalistic style

INSPIRED BY NATURE, gardens created in the Naturalistic style mirror wild landscapes, blending swathes of colourful flowers and textural grasses. Designs complement large, country gardens but can also provide solutions for smaller urban sites, using a palette of carefully chosen robust plants.

Evoking nature

Since their introduction in the early 1990s, naturalistic styles have been adopted by many designers and become mainstream in gardens large and small. 'New naturalism', as it is sometimes known, is a movement influenced by natural plant communities, particularly the steppe grasslands of central Europe and the American prairies, although temperate woodland, the Mediterranean garrigue and maquis, and the South African fynbos provide sources of inspiration in some designs. Meadow plantings are also popular, these flowery fields offering a solution for sunny gardens and orchards.

A recent cultural catalyst for the widespread adoption of naturalistic styles is public concern for society's disconnection from nature and disregard for the ecological well-being of the planet and sustainable use of its resources. Threats to wildlife have also fuelled momentum, as gardens are now seen as essential habitats, with exotic plants, as well as native species, identified as important nectar sources for pollinating insects. In addition, current thinking supports the more sustainable plantings typical of this style, which require less energy to maintain and the use of fewer or no pesticides.

Hallmarks of the style are drifts of flowering perennial plants that possess a wild, natural look. When massed together, they form ethereal dreamscapes of colour, often diffused with ornamental grasses, their plumes of filamentous flowers misting the effect, especially in late summer and autumn. The principle is to create stylised versions of natural plant communities, rather than slavishly copying them, which would be very difficult to achieve.

Designs are composed of plants that come from similar habitats around the world to those being evoked, which won't flop or need staking. The planting palette is tightly tuned to suit the physical soil conditions and scale of the garden, with larger, more vigorous varieties used in extensive schemes, and less aggressive, more demure plants employed for intimate assemblages in domestic spaces. Plant knowledge is the key, and the most successful schemes are generally designed by experienced practitioners.

Natural evolution

The Naturalistic movement has its roots in the Heempark at Amstelveen in Holland, developed by conservationist and author Jac P Thijsse in the first half of the 20th century. Thijsse was concerned about the loss of native Dutch flora and developed a series of public parks using these plants in extensive stylised plantings. Scientists and researchers also helped formulate a better understanding of how plants perform in communities. German botanist Richard

LEFT The wider landscape beyond this wild garden is reflected through relaxed use of perennials, such as fennel, alliums, and phlomis, and drifts of grasses.

DESIGN BY HELEN ELKS-SMITH

BELOW Echoes of the Mediterranean infuse a scheme of low evergreen shrubs, including artemisia and lavender.

DESIGN BY THOMAS HOBLYN

OPPOSITE, LEFT Sentinels of the upright grass Calamagrostis x acutiflora 'Karl Foerster' punctuate leafy ground cover.

DESIGN BY IAN KITSON

OPPOSITE, RIGHT Easy-care euphorbias, rosemary, sedum and blue Perovskia atriplicifolia throng a gravel pathway.

DESIGN BY ACRES WILD

Hansen developed the now-famous research gardens at Weihenstephan in Munich from 1947 and, with Friedrich Stahl, published the seminal study *Perennials and their Garden Habitats* in 1991. At the nearby Westpark, designer Rosemarie Weisse used these principles to transform a disused gravel pit in the 1980s.

Dutch designer, plantsman and pioneer of the naturalistic style, Piet Oudolf, popularised this form of planting in the late 1980s and 1990s, and introduced a range of exciting new varieties which he has used in many major projects, including the Highline in New York, Scampston in North Yorkshire, and Skärholmen in Sweden, as well as his own garden at Hummelo in the Netherlands. In the United States, the late landscape architects, James van Sweden and Wolfgang Oheme, are widely recognised as the founders of the new American garden style, which combines drought-tolerant perennials from the prairies to create sustainable naturalistic designs.

Developing the style

The term 'naturalistic' distinguishes this style from traditional, purely aesthetic designs, such as the herbaceous borders in country gardens. Instead of plants being ordered by height, with the tallest at the back and smallest in front, there is a diversity throughout the scheme, with the spires and plumes of tall plants emerging from a matrix of low-growing forms. The intention for the garden owner or visitor is to become immersed in the plantings, with informal pathways meandering or crisscrossing the floral spectacle, allowing plants to be viewed from different angles rather than from the front, like a picture in a gallery, as is the case with traditional borders.

The complement of plants also differs from the normal retinue of garden flora, with *Echinacea*, *Persicaria* and *Veronicastrum,* together with ornamental grasses, such as *Miscanthus*, *Molinia* and *Stipa,* playing a central role. While naturalistic landscapes are filled with flower colour from late spring to mid-autumn, in the colder months, the plants' structural shapes and textures take the lead, their sere stems and seedheads providing interest throughout late autumn and winter, when they form landscapes with a completely different character.

In shaded sites, multi-stemmed trees or large shrubs with their lower branches pruned away are used to imitate coppiced woodland, with carpets of shade-tolerant flowers decorating the ground beneath.

The style is constantly being permutated, with new ideas making regular appearances at influential design shows worldwide. Schemes can be contrasted with contemporary architectural features and geometric topiary, or constrained in beds in minimalist designs where the unfettered plantings add exuberant piquancy.

MEDITERRANEAN GARDENS

The favourable climate of countries bordering the Mediterranean has for centuries drawn people to this region and gardens that represent these fair weather provinces have become increasingly popular.

Plants from the Mediterranean and countries that share the same climatic conditions, including the Californian coast, southern Mexico and parts of South Africa, have evolved distinctive characteristics to cope with the aridity. Adaptations to drought include hairy or felted leaves, narrow or filigree foliage, and compact or slender habits, while many spring bulbs become dormant in summer to escape the heat. *Santolina*, lavender, *Cistus*, and *Agapanthus* hail from the Mediterranean, and thrive in full sun and the poor, dry soils typical of the region. Cool, wet winters and rich soil will cause these plants to die, but digging grit into clay or planting in raised beds to improve drainage will increase success rates.

To create that 'holiday abroad' ambience, designers often include planting from the Mediterranean around swimming pools and patio areas, while walls and raised beds are built from rough-hewn or knapped stonework to lend an authentic look. Laying gravel or pebbles over the soil also helps to evoke the arid landscape. Old, gnarled olive trees, imported from abandoned orchards, imbue settings with a sense of maturity and structure, while the hardier palm trees and potted citrus bushes, which are easily brought undercover in winter, enrich the planting designs.

Mediterranean planting decorates this design by Andy Sturgeon

Designing meadows

Popular features in many contemporary designs, meadows look spectacular in large, open gardens and orchards in countryside locations. Imposing when in full bloom and wildlife-friendly, meadows offer a design solution for gardens where regular lawn mowing is not economically sustainable or would be difficult because of the terrain, but where occasional rough cutting is feasible.

Some designers take a traditional approach and seek to emulate hay meadows, while others use Dr Nigel Dunnett's model to create 'Pictorial Meadows'. Dunnett has conducted groundbreaking research into plant communities at Sheffield University's Department of Landscape, and developed a range of annual and perennial seed mixes that offer cost-effective plantings with long flowering seasons that require minimal maintenance.

Exciting effects can also be created by exploiting the contrast between mown turf and meadow. For example,

LEFT A range of grasses, including closely mown turf, long grass with model sheep, and beds of barley, combine to create a dramatic textural carpet.

DESIGN BY ACRES WILD

ABOVE Ox-eye daisies thrive in the sunny spots in orchards.

DESIGN BY WILSON MCWILLIAM

BELOW Perennials and annuals combine in an explosion of colour.

DESIGN BY ARABELLA LENNOX-BOYD

Debbie Roberts and Ian Smith of Acres Wild have cut meadow plantings into geometric blocks, with mown pathways in between. Other designs include sinuous pathways meandering through a meadow of wild flowers to a secluded arbour, evoking a romantic idyll few can resist.

Wild flowers can be combined with more structural shrubs and trees to produce a range of exciting designs. Architectural box, holly or yew topiary dotted in swathes of wild flowers like giant chess pieces will create a dramatic picture, while obelisks made from metal or wood, supporting vigorous climbers such as roses, provide vertical punctuation points. You could also include modest plots of corn, paying homage to our agrarian culture – the contrast between architectural cubes of ripening corn and verdant mown turf creates a startling sight. In orchards, cowslips, primroses and red campion will cope with the dappled shade and draw in insects to pollinate the flowers and tree blossom.

Woodland edges

Native forest trees are supplemented with species such as Stewartia and Cercidiphyllum that offer different seasonal features.

Timber trail

A meandering weathered-timber pathway complements the planting, and blends effortlessly into the natural landscape.

CASE STUDY

DESIGN BY DAN PEARSON

A naturalistic garden

The Meadow Garden at the Tokachi Millennium Forest in Japan is composed of an intricate balance of shrubs and herbaceous perennials. Entrepreneur Mitsushige Hayashi developed the park to encourage a largely urbanised public to re-engage with the landscape and nature. Surrounded by forest and farmland at the foothills of the mountains, the growing season in this area is short, with snow in September and winter temperatures dipping to -25°C (-13°F). This garden is one of three developed by Dan Pearson on a five hectare site near the restaurant, and it is designed to provide a visual link with the landscape beyond. It combines a range of shrubs and 35,000 perennials that are related to and emulate the waves of plants that live together in the forest. The plants are mutually compatible, with balanced growth habits, and include tall species, such as *Persicaria*, *Eryngium* and *Miscanthus*, together with lower forms, including *Astilbe*, *Gillenia*, *Salvia* and *Veronica*.

DAN PEARSON

Trained at RHS Garden Wisley and the Royal Botanic Gardens, Kew, Dan became a garden and landscape designer in 1987. He has won a number of awards at the RHS Chelsea Flower Show. An early proponent of naturalistic planting and advocate of the use of local materials and techniques in tune with nature, 'place making' is a key part of his philosophy. Based in London, Dan has created projects in the UK and in Japan. He is also an author, ambassador for the Tree Council and a Royal Designer for Industry (RDI).

Water gardens

CALM AND REFLECTIVE or bold and dramatic, water creates a powerful effect, whatever the design intention. Use it to enliven a space with a cascade thundering into a pool below, or create a still pond fringed with plants or featuring a single water lily to convey a sense of peace and tranquillity.

Dramatic effects

Of all the features that can be included in a garden, water is the most powerful. One of the natural elements that collectively cradle human life, it is unsurprising that water has such a profound effect on our sense of wellbeing, compelling us to embrace all it has to offer. Creatively, it is the chameleon of the garden. Amorphous and fluid, water assumes both its shape and character from how it is used: dark and reflective, languid and romantic, playful and capricious, or dramatic and forceful, it conveys the style and tone of the garden's design. The sounds it produces are as diverse as its visual qualities, with notes ranging from high-pitched drips to a melodious gurgle and cacophonous crash.

Wherever water is located it will attract wildlife, helping us to connect with nature. While a splash pool will act as a welcome stop for passing birds, more permanent bodies of water will support complex and important ecosystems. Properly managed, even a small pond will become a significant nature reserve, especially when linked to other sites in the neighbourhood.

While water features are frequently included as incidental focal points, like pieces of sculpture, a water garden is any design where the ornamental or creative use of water predominates. Schemes can be culturally influenced by historical precedents to suit the architecture or landscape, or they may be contemporary, using this fluid medium to relay something new and distinctive. But even in modern gardens, water features are informed by techniques that were devised thousands of years ago. Many designers also draw on historic designs for inspiration, reinventing them using the latest materials, technologies and styling.

Water gardens through history

Water has been an integral part of garden design for many centuries. Essential to life, clean water is a precious commodity, especially where it is scarce in areas such as the Mediterranean region, Arabia and southern India. Deeply embedded in religious and social culture, its ornamental use was historically regarded as a privilege, reserved for the wealthiest in society.

Some of the first water gardens were created by the Chinese over 3,000 years ago. They evolved an asymmetric garden style, creating stylised evocations of the surrounding mountainous landscape, with rocks, trees and water laid out according to carefully devised rules and conventions. Japanese water gardens evolved from the Chinese style in the 9th and 10th centuries, and their influence is referenced in the work of many contemporary designers from both Asia and the West

A contemplative reflective pool of shallow water creates a moat around an intimate patio. A filtration system was fitted here to keep the water clean and clear, and to maintain the pebble effect.

DESIGN BY STUART CRAINE

who are drawn to their symbolism and celebration of the natural world.

The Italian Renaissance of the 16th century brought water gardens to life. Wealth and status was paramount during this period, and water features, such as the fabulous terraced water gardens of Villa D'Este, allowed the nobility to show off their power and influence. Likewise, the water features in the formal parterre gardens of 17th century France, such as Versailles and Vaux le Vicomte, were a demonstration of wealth and new technologies. Pools and fountains were used to contrast with the intricate patterns of clipped plants and fine statuary, creating a canvas of astonishing human endeavour when viewed from above.

As a reaction to the tightly controlled French style, the English landscape school of the 18th century sought to imitate nature. Landscape designer William Kent created romantic settings adorned with cascades, canals, rills

and lakes at Stowe in Buckinghamshire, while Lancelot 'Capability' Brown, influenced by Kent's designs, was famous for his grasslands punctuated by serpentine lakes.

Designing with water

The use of water should echo the style of your garden, with a single feature or assembly of smaller pools and cascades linked together to create a unified scheme, either filling the whole garden or an element in a larger concept. In many period gardens, water features are traditionally formal and geometrical in design close to the dwelling, becoming free-form or natural looking further from the house, but you do not have to follow this rule. A natural pond can complement a cottage or wildlife garden right next to the house, while a formal pond would inject a dramatic focal point when used to counterpoint meadow-style planting in a contemporary design. The hard landscaping and planting also influences

PARADISE GARDENS OF ANCIENT PERSIA

Often used as inspiration for contemporary water gardens, the paradise gardens of Persia date back to 400 BC. Their design is based on the pattern of irrigation channels, symbolically and physically representing water as the source of life. Four rills intersect in the centre of the garden, referencing the four rivers of life, with a fountain often set at the point where they meet. This style, along with Roman and other Islamic artistic influences, gave rise to the cloistered gardens in Spain, the most famous being Generalife and the Alhambra at Granada. Paradise gardens can be easily evolved to create beautiful courtyards in modern settings, the rills and fountains lending us the same sense of peace and tranquillity in our hot and dusty cities as they did thousands of years ago in the Middle East.

Cleve West's modern interpretation of a paradise garden

the character and personality of a water garden, with features surrounded by paving tending to look more formal than those edged with plants.

When creating water features that mimic nature it is best to locate them at the lowest point in the garden, just as you would see them in a natural landscape. Nothing is more alien than a pond sited where water has seemingly run up hill to fill it, unless it's perched in a recess in the landscape.

FAR LEFT Bisected by paving, a formal stepped rill creates drama and movement across the garden.

DESIGN BY SUE ADCOCK

LEFT A limpid pool shrouded by leafy plants forms an intimate retreat, with stepping stones allowing access to the water.

DESIGN BY ACRES WILD

ABOVE LEFT A sunken tank provides a crisp edge to an urban water feature. Echoing gardens in arid regions, the planting comprises leafy drought-tolerant species, such as euphorbia and iris, rather than marginal plants.

DESIGN BY JOE SWIFT

Creative lighting

Sprays of fibre optic cable with LED lighting at the tips provides the illusion of a nighttime firefly display along the deck edge.

Pond edging

Black painted blockwork disguises the pond liner and ensures a crisp edge. The water level is topped up automatically, maintaining an average depth of 90cm (36in).

Marginal planting

Continuous planting from beds below the water surface to the surrounding garden forms a seamless transition from pond to land.

Sinuous decking

The curved hardwood decking boards, used to construct the boardwalk, were machine-cut off site to create a perfect arc.

CASE STUDY

DESIGN BY IAN KITSON

A contemporary water garden

This country garden, designed by Ian Kitson with planting designs by Julie Toll, is adjacent to an east-facing property set up on a hill. The curvaceous free-form pool was created from an area that had previously been a tennis court, and, had the client not been brave enough to remove it, the potential for this lower part of the garden would never have been realised. The vision for the pool area was two-fold: firstly it needed to remain an integral part of the overall design language and character of the garden, and secondly, it had to act as a valuable wildlife habitat. The boardwalk is the culmination of a journey through the upper sunken gardens and naturalistic perennial plant displays, while the deck echoes the shape of the plant forms on the distant hills beyond the boundaries. The space provides a key vantage point, with views across colourful planting to the house, while the marginal plants merge into wild flower meadows that blend into the surrounding landscape.

IAN KITSON

Ian has been a garden designer since 1980, and holds qualifications in landscape architecture, architecture and the conservation of historic parks and gardens. He is also a Fellow and past chair of the Society of Garden Designers. His work is celebrated for its originality, and he has created award-winning schemes throughout the UK for private clients, as well as public bodies, often leading multi-disciplinary teams. He operates from studios in central London and Yorkshire.

An array of leafy plants, such as
Paulownia, hardy bananas and Arbutus
lend a subtropical air, while scarlet
Crocosmia 'Lucifer' adds floral zing
to this exotic-style design.

DESIGN BY LUCY SOMMERS

Subtropical style

FLAMBOYANT FOLIAGE, exotic colourful flowers and unfettered leafy lushness embody this style. The vogue for subtropical design has been propelled by the ease with which we can now visit inspiring new landscapes and emulate these exotic locations in our gardens at home.

Exotic inspirations

Subtropical-style gardens have long been celebrated in their native homelands, but they are increasingly becoming a possibility for many 21st century gardeners in cool climates, with cities providing the warmer microclimates needed for exotic plants to flourish. Relatively inexpensive air travel has also brought previously unattainable destinations to the masses, offering a wealth of inspiration. Drinking in the rich variety of landscapes and plants, and captivated by such unalloyed exoticism, we yearn for reminders at home, recreating far-flung landscapes either as entire gardens or a special element of the design. Creativity is only limited by the strength of your imagination.

Defining features of the subtropical style are large-leaved trees and shrubs, and brightly coloured flowers and foliage, which are combined to create jungle-like tapestries of shape, colour and texture. Water, in the form of limpid pools or noisy cascades, further enhances the desired ambience, with architectural structures, artefacts and ornaments helping to build the stage set. Sand, gravel and pebbles can be combined to create a beachside panorama, while grasses surrounded by leafy plantings suggest a forest clearing.

The influx of hardier plant selections from higher altitudes offers endless opportunity for enterprising gardeners to create something very different, yet more sustainable, in areas that suffer frosts. You can also infuse subtropical schemes with hardy plants that mimic those from warm, lush landscapes, such as the bold-leaved *Fatsia japonica* and many shrubby euphorbias. These evergreens offer year-round interest in gardens with an exotic theme, while hot-hued tender bedding plants illuminate them in summer. Subtropical-style designs are even possible in cold and windy sites, such as on roof gardens; designer Andy Sturgeon has used *Cordyline, Phormium* and tough grasses, including *Miscanthus*, on a London roof to convey the look.

Tropical traditions

The passion for exotic, tender plants dates back to the 19th century when species from warmer climates were first brought back to Europe. New technologies, including the invention of plate glass in the 1840s, fuelled interest in these plants and professional plant collectors were despatched to discover rare new orchids and other exotics to decorate the glass palaces that were being built at that time. Although many were thought to be tender when first cultivated, experiment and experience showed some to be hardy in Britain, or at least hardy enough to be placed outside for the summer. The first subtropical garden in the UK was built in London's Battersea Park by John Gibson in 1863. Gibson had previously been sent out to India to look for exotic novelties by the 3rd Duke of Devonshire and his then head gardener, Joseph Paxton. Entranced by what he saw, Gibson sought to create a subtropical display back home, assembling all manner of tender plants to form massed displays and weaving bedding plants into intricate mosaics, known as 'carpet bedding', a style which was then copied in parks and gardens throughout the land. Battersea's subtropical garden continued to enthrall visitors until World War II, but then fell into decline; friends of the Park revived the feature in 1994 and the restored garden is now open to the public.

Contemporary styling

The subtropical garden style has survived in various forms over the years, but has largely declined in public places due to the lack of professional staff to develop and maintain the displays and sweeping cuts to parks' budgets. However,

interest is still strong in private gardens, fuelled by the wide availability of 'exotic' plants, such as palms and evergreen trees and shrubs.

Carpet bedding has largely fallen out of fashion and has been superseded by a more naturalistic style that echoes wild and cultivated subtropical landscapes. Designers and home-owners have also taken advantage of the hardier forms of tender plants that are being introduced from previously unexplored areas, such as Northern Vietnam and Taiwan. These more durable plants, including hardy palms, such as *Trachycarpus*, shrubby trees like *Tetrapanax*, tree ferns (*Dicksonia antarctica*), and spiky succulents, including *Agave*, have opened up exciting new design possibilities, particularly in urban and coastal areas that enjoy milder winters. Inspiration can be gleaned from publically accessible gardens, such as Abbotsbury

LEFT A Mediterranean retreat is enlivened by colourful perennials and drought-tolerant shrubs, succulents and citrus trees.

ABOVE This secretive trail comprises leafy, shade-loving Fatsia, bamboos and tree ferns, and woodland perennials.

Subtropical Gardens in Dorset, Will Giles' remarkable Exotic Garden in Norfolk, and, the most famous example of all, Tresco Abbey Garden on the Isles of Scilly.

Dressing the set

While plants provide the ambience, buildings, furnishings and artefacts can reinforce the character of the subtropical style. You can create an eclectic look with elements from a variety of sources, or opt for a more carefully researched approach to create a colonial or more culturally indigenous theme. Many off-the-peg garden buildings with a verandah, railings, and either a tin shingle or thatched roof, are ideal for a colonial look. Or, if your budget will stretch, why not go for bespoke architecture, such as a Thai dwelling on stilts? Dressing the set with appropriate artefacts will create a design that exudes charm. A beach-hut setting with a tin sheet or thatched roof, complete with typical *objets trouvés*, will lend bags of atmosphere, or simply include a few colourful soft furnishings coupled with modern furniture and tropical-style umbrellas to transform the commonplace into a subtropical paradise.

CREATING AN IDEAL MICROCLIMATE

The trick to creating a successful subtropical planting scheme in a less than favourable location is to identify an ideal microclimate, or an area where one can be successfully created. A 'microclimate' is a zone where the conditions differ from the general climatic characteristics and, in terms of subtropical planting, this may be an area of increased warmth, moisture or shelter. South or west-facing aspects are usually warmer than sites that face east or north, which are cool and exposed, and only suitable for durable, shade-tolerant plants. Some tender plants' ability to survive can be determined by an increase of just one or two degrees, so placing them in a slightly warmer site can make all the difference. You can also grow plants from drier climates, such as succulents and bulbs, in areas that experience low air temperatures, if their rootstocks are not saturated by cold winter rain.

There are many ways to improve your conditions and widen your plant choice. Try erecting walls and fences to trap warm air; brick walls also radiate heat and raise the temperature further. Or plant hedgerows or groups of trees and shrubs along exposed boundaries to provide shelter, and if you have heavy clay soil, plant exotics in raised beds filled with free-draining soil mixed with horticultural grit. Whatever your conditions, there are subtropical-style plants to suit; your designer or plant supplier will be able to advise you further.

Denise Cadwallader's contemporary exotic-themed garden

Encroaching jungle

Mass plantings of trees, bamboos and leafy shrubs merge the garden with the neighbouring properties behind, creating the impression of an encroaching jungle.

Casual furniture

Rustic hardwood furniture and a calico parasol create a beach-side atmosphere, while fixed benches define the patio edge.

Weatherworn decking

Naturally weathered boards create the impression of an abandoned 'forgotten world' and provide a foil for the planting.

Exotic-style planting

Hardy, yet exotic-looking plants, such as *Trachycarpus* and *Chamaerops* palms, *Phormium* and *Kniphofia* lend a flamboyant look.

Effective edging

The undulating, mounding habit of the evergreen shrub *Hebe rakaiensis* makes it ideal for hiding the edges of timber steps.

CASE STUDY

DESIGN BY ACRES WILD

A tropical-style garden

The design brief for this garden was to exploit the 50m x 25m (165ft x 82ft) sloping site behind a modest brick house in southern England, creating two functional spaces: one for dining, the other for entertaining and sunbathing. The seating area was also designed to offer views of a stream that runs along the edge of the slope. The original garden comprised a lawn with fringing borders and crumbling stone retaining walls. The solution was to create decked and paved terraces, supported by serpentine retaining walls, with a lawn below leading to a board walk beside the stream. The subtropical planting includes chusan palms (*Trachycarpus fortunei*), the European fan palm (*Chamaerops humilis*), tree ferns (*Dicksonia antarctica*), *Miscanthus floridulus* grasses, and a range of bamboos and spiky phormiums. Hummocks of box and *Hebe rakaiensis* spill over the timber decking, while red-hot pokers and the daylily *Hemerocallis* 'Stafford' provide floral highlights.

ACRES WILD

Debbie Roberts and Ian Smith both trained in Landscape Architecture at Leeds University but elected to focus on garden design, forming Acres Wild in 1988. Most of their award-winning designs are for gardens in country settings, but they also work in other styles and situations. Their design philosophy is to integrate the house with the garden, creating a strong underlying structure softened with naturalistic planting. Based in Sussex, their work includes projects in the UK, Europe, and the United States.

GARDEN GALLERY

ARCHITECTURAL IDEAS

Practically every successful garden has architectural elements embedded in it, performing a whole host of roles. In its widest sense architecture is used to provide the structure or bones of a design in which other elements sit. These various built structures may be the focus and on show all the time or, conversely, they may be subtle and only apparent in the depths of winter. It is the intriguing way that all the elements relate to each other creating an alchemy of effects that raises a garden from the prosaic to something special.

In this chapter we explore ways in which architecture and architectural elements can be used to best effect through the creative eyes of different designers, using a wide spectrum of materials and evolving technologies.

In 'Defining spaces' we present solutions for boundaries and internal divisions within gardens of all sizes and styles. 'Making an entrance' provides a portfolio of ideas for entering or passing between spaces, illustrating how character can be defined through architectural detailing. 'Journeys and routes' defines how we move around the garden and explore its attractions. Decorating and personalising outdoor spaces is essential and 'Ornamental flourishes' displays a gallery of artworks, ranging from the monumental to the poignant and amusing. Lighting can transform a garden in exciting ways to enhance its atmosphere, and 'Dramatic illumination' shows how daytime experiences can turn into night-time theatre at the flick of a switch. Finally, 'Inspirational water' studies an element central to garden design for centuries, showing its astonishing versatility and contribution to wildlife and the environment.

LEFT The bold, clean lines of a formal rill contrast dramatically with the landscape beyond, while the grassy planting mimics the surrounding arable countryside.
DESIGN BY SUE ADCOCK

BELOW A rigid forest of horsetail stems, their invasive roots contained in a trough, flank a ghostly mesh sculpture, adding character to the formal setting.
DESIGN BY ANTHONY PAUL

Defining spaces

WHATEVER YOUR GARDEN'S size or shape, it will be defined by boundaries and open spaces, such as patios and terraces, that confine and shape the design, while the materials and styles used convey character and mood.

Beautiful boundaries

All gardens are determined by boundaries that govern the size and shape of the space. Walls, fences, and hedges are used to denote the extent of the legal ownership of land, but boundaries also offer exciting opportunities for innovative design. They influence how the garden interacts with the surrounding landscape, and can be used to control views in and out of the space. You may want to block unsightly structures, for example, or create privacy with screens or hedges, while leaving other boundaries open to capture attractive panoramas or landmarks. Barriers also help to control climate, with rows of trees and shrubs or perforated screens providing shelter from prevailing wind. In addition, you can use screens to subdivide your space, creating rooms or apportioning areas for various functions. Boundaries are often the first elements we see when entering a garden, so consider them carefully in relation to the design as a whole.

> *"The design of boundaries in small gardens is crucial as they are permanently on show. Natural materials, such as western red cedarwood or old bricks, look beautiful in traditional and modern gardens, or try smooth rendered brick with a dark finish, which recedes into the background and contrasts well with green foliage."*
> CHARLOTTE ROWE

1 Slatted screens in western red cedarwood provide an elegant boundary screen for a garden with an awkward change in level. Affording privacy and filtering wind, it is practical yet beautiful.

DESIGN BY CHARLOTTE ROWE

2 Raw concrete screens stencilled with a potent script provide an uncompromising contemporary barrier.

DESIGN BY JAMES BASSON

3 Mellow dry stone walls afford a timeless solution for a boundary or internal screen, and blend seamlessly into country settings.

DESIGN BY MANDY BUCKLAND

4 A gallery of rusted corten steel panels, softened by foliage spilling through them, form screens to divide up the garden space.

DESIGN BY SARA JANE ROTHWELL

5 The bold patterning of this tiny courtyard plays with perspective as metallic strips continue the patio design up a boundary wall.

DESIGN BY PAUL HENSEY

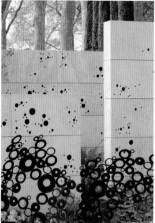

1 Elevated or stilt hedging provides privacy and shelter.

2 Interposed panels of decorated marble allow access while providing both a focal point and visual barrier.

DESIGN BY ANDY STURGEON

3 A circular lawn draws the eye to the captured view of the landscape.

DESIGN BY ACRES WILD

Boundaries are either imposed or self-determined, a distinction that may influence your approach. Legal boundaries require permanent installations, such as walls or durable fences, for security, but even here opportunities for creative design abound, such as the use of materials that reflect the local or historical character of the site, anchoring the garden into its landscape. If boundaries are on show, it pays to invest in good quality materials that will create a visual asset and can stand alone, rather than structures that require camouflaging with planting or paint.

In urban or densely populated areas, privacy may be a key requirement, with elevated boundaries providing refuge. Where space is at a premium, 'pleached' hedges or trellis screens clad with climbers can be accommodated in a small area to provide shelter or block out unsightly views.

The garden's prevailing climate and geographical location may also determine the nature of the boundary treatment. Exposed sites battered by winds may need stronger structures than elsewhere, or the development of a shelterbelt of trees and shrubs to help dissipate the wind and provide a comfortable space for seating and more sensitive plants.

You can also direct attention onto a 'borrowed' landscape or distant feature, such as a church steeple, by leaving gaps in a boundary structure and thereby leading the eye to the focal point. Alternatively, panoramic views can be left open by employing historical tricks such as the 'ha ha' – a 'v' shaped ditch that runs along the perimeter, popular in the 18th century, or the use of simple stock-proof fencing.

Architectural railings can be used to create a similar effect in urban gardens that look out onto a cityscape. If space allows, boundaries may dissipate into the surrounding landscape through trees or hedgerows.

Dividing spaces

Internal boundaries need not be as substantial as external barriers, becoming more notional, and indicating change rather than imposing it. Barriers can be low or see-through, using trellises, coloured Perspex or toughened glass panels to break up the space. Formally or irregular clipped hedges also provide structural barriers that can effectively separate garden spaces. Or you can have fun playing with barriers that selectively open and close views into spaces as you move around the garden, thereby increasing the element of surprise and intrigue, and helping to draw the visitor through the landscape.

GREEN WALLS

An increasing number of gardens now include green wall technology as part of the design. When properly considered and carefully installed they are a real asset, creating visually attractive solutions for disguising and softening unsightly surfaces and structures.

Fuelling these features is concern for the environment, particularly in urban areas. Greening walls helps to reduce the 'heat-island' effect by lowering ambient temperatures and moderating energy gains and losses from buildings. It also helps to reconnect us with nature and create new habitats for wildlife.

Greening walls is more than growing climbers over the surface, and it is always wise to seek advice from experts before installing a green wall to ensure the best results. The drive is to establish self-contained communities of plants in modular growing systems that can be attached to any vertical surface. Systems vary in sophistication, from the simplest synthetic fabric or plastic mesh bags to professional systems with computer-controlled

water and feeding mechanisms. The fabric or plastic mesh bags are filled with compost, and then either directly attached to the wall surface or fixed to a framework. They are watered manually or irrigated using reservoir or automated drip-watering systems, gravity-fed by collected rainwater or the mains supply. Professional systems use moulded plastic hoppers with capillary matting and substrates to support plant growth. Automatic watering and feeding mechanisms enable water to percolate evenly to all the plants, with water residues either going to drainage or being recycled. Rainwater is also harvested to supplement mains water.

Plants for long-term displays need to be tolerant to drought, intense sunlight or shade, depending on the location of the wall, and possess a clumping or slowly creeping habit that won't swamp neighbours. Evergreen leaves will also maintain the display. Many green wall plants, such as ferns, *Heuchera* and *Euonymus*, come from woodlands, while others, including *Bergenia*, *Erigeron* and *Festuca*, are from rockier open habitats.

1 Evergreen heuchera, ferns, sedges and bergenia create interest year round.

DESIGN BY PATRICIA FOX

2 A selection of foliage plants creates a tapestry of colour and texture in this small urban garden.

DESIGN BY MANDY BUCKLAND

3 Luxuriant leaves in the green wall blend with the groundcover planting below.

DESIGN BY PAUL HENSEY

"When selecting plants for a green wall, it's essential to remember the adage, 'right plant right place'. Check the light and wind conditions carefully and seek advice from green wall experts on the plants you have chosen, since some can grow very differently in a wall compared to a traditional bed."

PATRICIA FOX, ARALIA DESIGN

1 The various orientations and natural grain of the timber slats on the seating and decking create a striking, elegant ambience on this city roof garden.

DESIGN BY CHARLOTTE ROWE

2 Mellow stone paviors make an understated yet timeless contribution to this sunken patio in a country garden.

DESIGN BY ACRES WILD

3 Natural materials, such as timber decking, gravel and cobbles, chime with a casual array of cubed timber seats, which are functional as well as decorative.

DESIGN BY ANDY STURGEON

4 A series of plinths, each formed from a mosaic of paviors, seem to float on the water that runs between them.

DESIGN BY LOUISE HARRISON-HOLLAND

Designing patios and terraces

Patios and terraces form the social hub of the garden, and are an essential ingredient of any design. The terms patio and terrace are often used interchangeably, but a terrace is generally considered to be an area of hard standing attached to a building and traditionally raised above ground level, although it can also be a paved roof garden. A patio is any hard-paved social space located anywhere in the garden. When considering their design, decide what activities and functions you want your socialising areas to embrace, particularly if space is at a premium.

Location of any type of patio is key. Most are outdoor extensions of indoor spaces, such as the kitchen, and located next to the house, affording a direct connection with the facilities inside. Aspect is another important consideration, with protection from wind just as important as access to sunlight. Make use of the protection buildings provide, or create shelter with planting or perforated screens that will slow down the wind without causing turbulence, and cool sunny spaces with canopies, pergolas or trees, such as maples or birches that cast dappled shade. If your house is north facing and in permanent shade, try a patio at the end of your plot where it will be sunnier, or design a series of areas around the garden to catch the sun as it tracks through the sky. Also apportion sufficient hard standing for seating and dining sets, allowing at least twice the area of the table to enable chairs to be moved out easily. Permanent cooking areas will also need a paved space around them, while a built-in canopy will shelter them from rain and snow in winter.

Ensure the materials used for a patio or terrace are durable and non-slip, particularly if the site is shaded. Flat, even surfaces are needed for alfresco dining areas; paving or decking, rather than gravel or grass, are good choices for these spaces, but remember that wood can be slippery when wet, unless it has a grooved surface or other textured finish.

1 A series of simple arches can provide a modest entranceway or herald a change of direction. The fast-growing hop, Humulus lupulus 'Aureus', offers a leafy cover.

DESIGN BY PATRICIA FOX

2 An intricate antique metal gate, supported by warm-toned dry stone columns, makes a grand and imposing gesture, offering hints of what may be experienced in the garden beyond.

DESIGN BY CLEVE WEST

3 Formally marking the transition between two spaces, a simple brick arch is enlivened by tile inserts and a contrasting central keystone.

4 Integral with the boundary wall, an archway invites entry, while a short flight of steps suggests a garden of high status.

DESIGN BY ACRES WILD

5 Positioned inside a generous archway, a timber gate allows a tantalising glimpse into the garden and offers a sense of enclosure and protection.

DESIGN BY ANTHONY PAUL

6 A Gothic arbour frames the main vista through the design, creating a welcome opportunity to linger and appreciate the scene.

DESIGN BY JOHN BROOKES

Making an entrance

FIRST IMPRESSIONS are critical to any design, and features that mark the entrance to a garden are particularly important, reflecting its character and ambience, defining the route into the space and offering visitors a hint of what lies beyond the threshold.

Points of entry

Design elements that contribute to our enjoyment and the value of a garden always require careful consideration and entranceways are a case in point. Often the first elements we encounter, they control our entry into a garden, but can be far more than just a physical barrier restricting unauthorised access. When carefully designed, they provide tantalising glimpses of the garden beyond. They may also be imposing, making a grand gesture, or understated, creating a surprise when we discover what lies ahead, while ornamentation can introduce or perpetuate a style or personalised theme.

In any garden, there needs to be a hierarchy of entranceway solutions, from the main gateway to interior openings within the space. These are determined by a variety of intentions and purposes that help to enrich the fabric of the design. The scale and proportion of the entranceway and the way it is framed with lintels, archways or other architectural decoration can imbue a sense of importance and authority, while the use of different paving materials at the point of entry further enforces a change of status or demarcation from one area to another. Conversely, an understated gap in a wall, fence or hedge allows the design to flow between two spaces in a more casual way, discrete and unannounced, and offers the chance to create surprise with a dramatic view or focal point beyond the threshold. Context and the geographical location are other important factors to consider. For example, simple, rustic gates will look more appropriate than civic and elaborate features in gardens set in the countryside. If the design becomes more relaxed with distance from the house, then entranceways to those areas should, likewise, be more casual or practical in nature and meld into the landscape. Hewn stone uprights are likely to be all that is required to mark the entrance to a wild garden or meadow from a formally planted area, or an archway set into trellis screens could be used in a small suburban garden.

Designing with gates and doors

The design of a door or gateway will help augment or reinforce the intention of the design. A solid door set into a wall will impart the look of a secret garden, remote and private, forever willing us to enter and discover something new. Perforated or open-structured gates and doors offer glimpses into the space beyond, still beckoning us to enter, but secure in the knowledge of what we will find there. Such solutions can be used to enhance a vista, enabling views from one end of the garden to the other, with aligned entranceways guiding the visitor through a series of outdoor rooms.

Gate design may also embody the theme of the design, making historical, cultural, artistic or personal references. It can be authoritarian, playful or whimsical in character and it is worth considering gates that are locally handcrafted to create an individual or quirky look or to enforce a particular cultural ideal that references the overall design. Alternatively, scour architectural salvage yards or internet sites for old or antique gates and doors that can be recycled to convey a period feel or individual approach, but ensure they are fit for purpose before making your purchase.

The colour and texture of a door or gate will also play an important role in the design. Rusted metal, such as corten steel, or weathered timber will deliver a sense of timelessness

1 Imposing slatted gates with a distinctive leaf motif announce entry to the walled kitchen garden at Gresgarth Hall in Lancashire.

DESIGN BY ARABELLA LENNOX-BOYD

2 Timber gates and a rose-clad arbour mark this entrance, allowing views of the meadow beyond.

DESIGN BY ANNE KEENAN

3 Suspense and mystery are heightened as visitors approach the narrow entrance to this secret garden, with the substantial antique door adding period charm.

DESIGN BY ACRES WILD

and stylish decay and if constructed from durable materials, such as oak or wrought iron, they are also likely to need little maintenance. Use of strong colour, such as red or yellow will command attention, while pastels or neutral shades – avoid white, which can be quite startling – will look more natural and fade into the distance.

"An effective way of bringing visual drama into gardens large and small is to use a device such as a moongate, which is a round opening, or an archway. By dividing the space or framing a view in such a way, you are focusing the eye and inviting people to explore the delights beyond."
ANA SANCHEZ-MARTIN

Sculptural garden opening by Ana Sanchez-Martin

Journeys and routes

PATHS AND STEPS create journeys through the garden, guiding visitors and helping to control their experience of the different spaces, with broad pathways promoting a leisurely stroll, and twists and turns or a change in level forcing them to stop and consider a view or feature.

Designing a pathway

Just as boundaries define and delineate spaces, pathways connect key elements and facilities together, while also enabling movement through the space. The design of any pathway is determined by the status, function and position of the features that need to be accessed, the amount and type of traffic each route will receive and the characteristics of the site. Fundamental elements of any garden scheme, the way in which pathways flow and perform influences how we interact with and enjoy the spaces they link together, and their design therefore requires careful consideration.

The quickest route between two points is a straight line and this may be required for practical purposes or for impact when the path is punctuated by a striking focal point. A meandering route, on the other hand, allows for more lingering experiences of flowering plants and views

> "A long, thin garden can feel like a corridor – the eye and the foot will travel quickly from one end to the other. To avoid this, use some indirect routes that travel across the garden to slow the pace, and make the space feel much wider too. You will find this allows you to create new vistas and enjoy every aspect of the garden."
>
> ANNE KEENAN

1 Informal pathways composed of hoggin (clay, sand and gravel bound together), suit country settings perfectly.
DESIGN BY JAMES SCOTT

2 The contoured design of this footpath impels us on, yet allows casual exploration of adjacent lawns and planting.
DESIGN BY IAN KITSON

3 Gravel is among the most flexible and cost-effective surfacing materials for pathways, allowing plants to encroach and blur the edges.
DESIGN BY ARABELLA LENNOX-BOYD

of incidental or surprise elements, such as sculpture, water features or seating. However, nothing is more frustrating than negotiating a meandering path when the route should be more direct, and most designers would also guard against overly complex routes.

Consider the width

Paving width is critical when designing paths and this again is determined by use. For example, narrow, meandering paths are difficult for wheelbarrows, mowers and other equipment to negotiate, and the planting on either side will soon make the passageway unnavigable. Ideally, paths should be wide enough for two people to pass by comfortably, usually about 0.9–1.2 (3–4ft), but 0.6m (2ft) may be sufficient for a simple track through planting.

Using two or three paving materials and playing with the width and proportion of the pathway can create a spectrum of design statements. Subtle or dramatic, these can help to forge character into a landscape or create optical effects, such as using contrasting bands of paving materials to break up long expanses, or creating a pausing point with a contrasting paving material where pathways intersect.

4 Changing the paving palette at key points creates visual variety or denotes a different status or use.

DESIGN BY ANNE KEENAN

5 Mown turf pathways are an easy and dramatic way to carve routes through meadows and wild gardens.

DESIGN BY ACRES WILD

6 Elevated timber boardwalks offer exciting opportunities to meander over wet and boggy ground.

DESIGN BY NIGEL PHILIPS

CHOOSING MATERIALS FOR PATHS AND STEPS

Materials for paths and steps can range from turf and loose or fixed gravel through to bricks and paviors. Turf will require regular mowing and maintenance to keep it in good condition, but it's cheap to install and useful for extensive spaces. Gravel and crushed stone is an effective fluid paving material that can be shaped and will flow like turf, but without the need to mow. Local gravels and stones lend regional character, while other aggregates can offer a variety of different colours and textures. Gravel is also an excellent foil for plants, ornaments and artefacts. Self-binding gravel or aggregate and clay mixes such as hoggin, which comprises dust-like and larger particles that are compressed to form a permeable, weed-free surface, are ideal for lightly trafficked country settings, while gravels sealed with resin offer a hard-wearing surface, suitable for heavily used or more urban and civic situations.

Slabs, bricks and concrete are good choices for the primary routes through the garden. Their high cost is offset by long-term durability and the visual quality they can bring. While recycled Yorkstone paving, antique brick or marble offer timeless elegance, paths created from reconstituted crushed stone and concrete can be just as effective and cheaper, with a bewildering range of textures, colours and shapes on offer. Sealed surfaces will require laying to falls to drains or soakaways, so that rainwater does not collect, resulting in hazards or flooding.

CLOCKWISE FROM TOP LEFT: Dark cobbles create fluid patterns; clay hoggin secured between granite sett edgings; elongated grey slates create motion; a rustic boardwalk effortlessly traverses a stream; sawn stone strips dramatically contrast with gravel and cobble infill.

1 Timber sleeper edgings backfilled with gravel are easy to install and provide an inexpensive and dynamic method of creating steps.

DESIGN BY ACRES WILD

Step designs

Navigating a change in level often requires the use of steps. There are recognised architectural specifications for steps' height (risers) and depth (treads) for ease of use and comfort; a proportion of 7-11 is often specified, which relates to a maximum riser height of 17.7cm (7in) and tread width of 27.9cm (11in), although this is a guide, not a hard and fast rule. Rest areas are best included every 18 steps, for every 1.2m (4ft) in height, or where there is a change in direction. Also ensure paving materials are secure and provide good traction, and shed water to prevent flooding or ice forming in winter. Steps also help impart a style or look. Wide steps are welcoming and give an impression of permanence and grandeur, and are easy to traverse; narrow steps can be used to accentuate a gradient, particularly if they also change direction to navigate the slope.

2 Rough-hewn irregular slate steps contrast with crafted mellow stone walls to create visual impact.

DESIGN BY JULIE TOLL

3 A flight of wide turf steps edged with stone allows the lawn to infuse the landscape, conveying a subtle change in level.

DESIGN BY SARA JANE ROTHWELL

4 Powerful yet elegant, these steps collect users from a wide terrace and direct them to a single point of entry.

DESIGN BY DOUGLAS COLTART

1 A bold backdrop made from silvery aluminium cylinders creates a lively, yet understated, rhythmic pattern, which is matched by the fresh green tones of shade-tolerant plants.

DESIGN BY ANDY STURGEON

2 Personalising a space is a key objective when decorating a garden, with humour often playing an important role. Here a pair of penguins are forever about to take a dip in an icy pool.

DESIGN BY DEAKINLOCK

3 While figurative sculpture can help humanise a garden, select a piece with care so that it suits the style and ambience of your space.

DESIGN BY ANTHONY PAUL

4 Referencing the spiritual cultures of other civilisations can exert a powerful force. This Meta Sudans or 'sweating cone' – a stone fountain of ancient Rome – is recreated in a woodland glade.

DESIGN BY ARABELLA LENNOX-BOYD

5 Simple yet dramatic, a gigantic corten steel picture frame captures the tranquil landscape beyond and reflects the evolving seasons.

DESIGN BY CHRIS ZBROZYNA

Ornamental flourishes

SCULPTURE AND ORNAMENT can be used to create exciting, dramatic effects in the garden: punctuating vistas with bold focal points, adding pathos or humour to the design or, when hidden in planting or an enclosed space, conveying surprise and intrigue.

Effects with sculpture and ornament

Gardens are a living art form that evolves and matures over time, and as an expression of our creativity, it is perhaps only fitting that we include more permanent ornamental features to decorate and personalise our outdoor spaces. Ornamentation can influence the ambience and atmosphere of a garden and what we choose and how we use it can affect our state of mind, as well as projecting our creative intent.

Sculpture and ornament is highly personal and multivarious: it may be obscure, obvious, practical or indulgent, or an interplay between all these things. It also sets the tone of the garden, be that light-hearted, capricious, amusing or deeply symbolic, and when used sequentially it may also tell a story or commemorate a person or event. Decorative nuances can be integral and woven into the fabric of the design, the creative threads released through bespoke

"The setting is key to choosing a sculpture. In general, figurative pieces, made form natural materials such as wood or stone, suit country settings, while urban gardens lend themselves to modern abstract sculptures made from metal or glass. But there are no definite rules and you often just have to go with your instincts."

ANTHONY PAUL

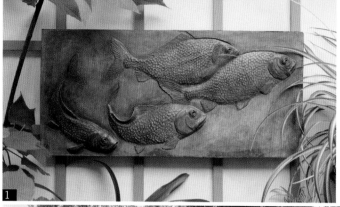

SCULPTING MATERIALS AND COLOURS

The materials from which artworks are created can influence the sense of place. Organic materials, such as wood, look soft and natural and are ideal for informal designs, while metals, including bronze, copper and iron, are more imposing, engendering a greater sense of permanence. Allowing metals such as cast iron to rust will imbue a patina of age and reflect the passage of time, but beware, they may also stain the setting on which the artwork stands.

Stone can be impassive or impersonal, yet it is also sublimely timeless and tactile. When roughly hewn and raw, it can echo a rugged landscape, but when intricately carved and sculpted, stone can also represent the most delicate forms.

Colour exerts a powerful influence on our perception of the garden and can be used through ornamental pieces to embellish the design narrative or create drama. But unless it forms part of the design intention, colour should be used sparingly and with care. Single, soft pastels sit more harmoniously in a garden setting than strong primaries, although these too can have a place, especially when used in contemporary gardens to create a focal point.

1 Thematic plaques, like this fish by Lucy Smith, make dramatic focal points.

2 Siting sculpture is as important as the subject of the piece itself, as these fluid figures floating over colourful country-style planting illustrate.

3 By capturing the surrounding landscape and reflecting light a mirrored finish dissipates the mass of an object, creating an eye-catching optical illusion.

DESIGN BY JOHN WYER

4 Simple shapes with clean lines often have the greatest impact, such as in the subtle interplay of size and colour in this arrangement of granite spheres.

DESIGN BY MANDY BUCKLAND

Lifesize horse made from recycled fencing wire, by Laura Antebi

artwork; conversely, art may be introduced for its own sake, to be savoured and admired in a setting of its own.

You can also use sculpture and art to create surprise, providing unexpected treats as you experience the garden, or they can act as triumphal statements, creating the main focal point of a design or the climax of the journey. The setting or staging is often as important as the artwork itself, which is why it's best to design in ornamental features at the outset, when they can be given due emphasis and space, rather than placing them retrospectively.

Ornamental options

Sculpture is the most popular form of garden ornament and may be abstract, capturing a mood or making an emotional or cultural statement, or figurative, representing a person or animal. Figurative pieces can sometimes be more difficult to place, as they bring a definite character and personality to the space that is unchanging and does not invite the freedom of interpretation that, say, an abstract piece of sculpture allows.

Friezes offer a potent way of bringing decoration into the garden, either as incidental elements or focal points. They are particularly useful in small gardens, where even a large, dramatic frieze can be accommodated, as they take up relatively little ground space. Shapes may be simple, superimposed geometrical forms or figurative work in bas relief, while mirrored elements can help enliven dark spaces by reflecting light and creating incident.

Objets trouvés, such as shells, driftwood or even old kitchen utensils, offer the opportunity to include highly personalised elements that recall memorable experiences or associations with loved ones, or they may be simply captivating objects in themselves. They can be tucked into alcoves, hung from branches, or casually placed along paths or in plantings to enhance the design.

1 When carefully considered from the outset, creative lighting allows you to extend the time you spend in the garden and provides endless exciting visual experiences.

DESIGN BY MANDY BUCKLAND

2 By underlighting a block table and slatted timber seat, this intimate urban garden takes on a completely different persona at night, with objects appearing to float as the sun sets and the lighting dominates.

DESIGN BY CHARLOTTE ROWE

Dramatic illumination

SENSITIVELY DESIGNED lighting schemes can transform a daytime garden into a magical, mysterious landscape at night, illuminating features such as trees and ornaments, while also lighting the way and allowing safe passage through the space after dark.

Lighting designs

Modern gardens are expected to serve and entertain their owners throughout the year and at most times of the day and evening, making lighting key to their effectiveness. Functional, practical and decorative, lighting can transcend the ordinary and commonplace with designs of real beauty and imagination. By highlighting or embellishing what is already there, a daytime scene can be transformed into a magical landscape, either unifying and simplifying the design intent or morphing it into something dramatically different.

Lights can distort or create new spatial relationships between various features and alter the way we perceive them and the spaces they inhabit. They also draw emotional responses like no other medium and offer opportunities to engage with the garden when we may not be able to

3 Subtle and understated illumination of particular objects, such as sculpture or architectural plants, often elicits a far more powerful effect than when the whole garden is saturated in light.

DESIGN BY CLEVE WEST

4 The stone pillars of a pergola are transformed into a powerful stage set through use of strong uplighting and by bathing the distant focal point in a contrasting beam of light.

DESIGN BY ANDREW FISHER TOMLIN

5 Dramatic lighting in brilliant colours can make an arresting sight, transforming our daytime appreciation of the space and the features within it.

DESIGN BY JANINE PATTISON

6 LED lighting can be used to highlight sudden changes in level and other potential hazards, while also providing opportunities for creating a range of decorative and colourful effects.

DESIGN BY TINA VALLIS

> *"Introducing coloured lighting into a garden adds drama but it needs to be carefully considered. Features such as water, textured walls, and large leaved plants lend themselves to coloured lights, and if you opt for RGB LED colour-change fittings you can alter the hues depending on the mood and effects you require."*
>
> JANINE PATTISON

get outside, such as in winter. Lighting also commands attention, particularly when used sparingly and with conviction. A single source can draw attention to a distant object or focal point and, by careful control of the way it is lit, foreshorten or extend our perception of distance. When lit, footpaths that lead to these objects are also invested with a status that may not be apparent in the day time. Features such as raised planting beds can be underlit to create the illusion that they are floating, while the intricate tracery of branches, rugged texture of brickwork and luscious curves of sculpture can all be accentuated when bathed in light.

Coloured lighting is another effective design tool, and can be used to spotlight particular aspects of the garden scene. Rather than creating the visual chaos of a seaside resort display, choose one or two complementary colours that work well together. Lighting units (LEDs) that alternate between colours can also be used to convey a variety of moods or ambience, with the sequencing programmed and controlled electronically.

Forward planning

While some types of lighting, such as gas lights or solar powered units, can be introduced retrospectively, most requires planning into the fabric of the design and commissioned as an integral part of the architecture. A particular vision may need bespoke solutions to create the special effects you have in mind, and a garden designer or specialist lighting company will be able to undertake the work to ensure it is safely and correctly installed. Ensure the specialist or electrician that installs your garden lighting is registered with one of the following governing bodies: NAPIT, ELECSA, ECA, or NICEIC. These ensure the contractor installs to BS7671 (the electrical regulations) and meets the necessary building regulations.

1 Take time to research all the various lighting systems available to achieve the effect you want. Here a stand-alone neon tube emits an eerie glow, bathing the area in an intimate light.

DESIGN BY ANDY STURGEON

2 Small yet powerful LEDs and an illuminated strip draw the eye to a trio of slender pots in this city garden, creating a dominant focal point when night falls.

DESIGN BY CHARLOTTE ROWE

3 Lights set into a deck pinpoint the edge, allowing safe passage through the garden, while the pool creates a sea of colourful light in the centre of the space.

DESIGN BY JOHN NASH

4 A clean white beam directed onto a cascade, fountain or water blade makes a dynamic night-time feature and throws spangles of light into the garden.

DESIGN BY ANDREW FISHER TOMLIN

LIGHTING OPTIONS

CONVENTIONAL LIGHTING SYSTEMS
Traditional mains-powered systems can produce light in a wide range of colours and intensities, and recent developments have made them safer and more efficient: bright halogen incandescent bulbs and the more efficient compact fluorescent lights use 75 per cent less power to produce the same effects as traditional incandescent light bulbs. Various types are available for different purposes, so evaluate which is best suited to your needs.

SOLAR POWER
The effectiveness of low voltage lighting powered by solar energy is dependent on the availability of sunlight and the battery capacity, although modern devices are improving all the time. Fairly cheap to buy, with no complicated or professional installation required, solar lights are ideal for casual illumination, decorative effects and powering novelty items. However, they are not suitable for safety features, such as lights for illuminating steps.

LEDS
LED lamps use Light Emitting Diodes instead of standard filaments or discharge lamps to provide the light source. They are considered to be the most environmentally sound lighting method, using only 10 per cent of the power needed by a standard incandescent bulb, with a lifetime of up to 50,000 hours and low surface temperature. Ideal for recessing into walls, decking, and driveways, they are useful for illuminating stairways and for producing underwater effects. Initial costs are higher than other forms of lighting, but LEDs are safe and very efficient. Bright white LEDs give a stark effect, while warm white and other colours produce softer, less intense illumination.

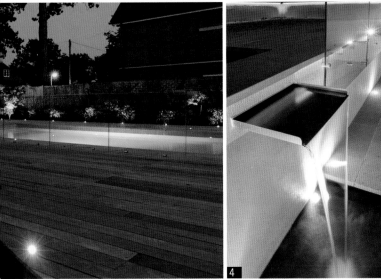

Inspirational water

BRINGING SPARKLE and sound to your garden, water can energise a design with splashing symphonies from fountains and cascades; increase light by mirroring the sky; or infuse a design scheme with quiet calm from a reflective pool or a wildlife pond.

Watery effects

Water is one of the most life affirming and dynamic elements you can introduce into a garden and when used creatively with sensitivity, skill and panache, it is also one of the most potent. Water takes on different persona, depending on how and where it is used: formal, geometric pools and fountains can be serious and powerful; meandering streams and plant-filled ponds lend a serene and natural look. Moving water can be playful too. Jets and cascades sparkle with light and create a comforting sound, and they can be programmed to turn on unexpectedly, creating surprise and excitement. Agitated water produces ripples that transmit hypnotic movement, while water walls, with films of water running over textured backdrops, create glistening, sinuous patterns.

You can also use water to convey a mood or ambience. Features can be personal and intimate, such as a rill designed to drip into a hidden pool, or triumphal, with cascades thundering into plunge pools, gurgling and boiling amongst imposing sculpture or dramatic ornament. Still water is often used to enhance contemplative landscapes, the surface reflecting the surrounding world, or romantically capturing blue sky and scudding clouds. But when contained within a dark vessel, the water becomes quiet and mysterious, mirroring all, but communicating little.

1 A restless film of water flows over the textured base in this formal rill, creating a powerful, dynamic feature between the flight of steps and filling the garden with sound.

DESIGN BY JOHN WYER

2 A blade of water disturbs the reflective surface of a stylish contemporary formal pool designed to intersect with an intimate fern-edged patio.

DESIGN BY DENISE CADWALLADER

3 Recreating the ambience of a romantic past, the stone edging on this canal-like raised tank, planted with water lilies and irises, provides seating for conversation or quiet contemplation.

DESIGN BY NIGEL PHILIPS

4 As if defying the laws of physics, a granite pathway stretches across a small pool, the effect heightened by allowing water to penetrate between each sett.

DESIGN BY CLEVE WEST

5 Films of water glide effortlessly over the mirrored surface of this elegant feature into a pool below, creating impact and reflecting light into the intimate space.

DESIGN BY ANDREW FISHER TOMLIN

6 Mimicking wild landscapes, naturalistic pools should be located at the lowest point of the garden and reflect the contours of their surroundings. A bridge provides access and a key viewing point.

DESIGN BY JAMES SCOTT

1

2

1 By intercepting water from an adjacent building this rain-fed, richly planted pond is ideal for wildlife. Excess water flows into a nearby culvert.

DESIGN BY CHERYL CUMMINGS

2 The centrepiece of a period formal garden, this sunken water feature acts as a focal point, its mirrored surface reflecting the ever-changing sky.

DESIGN BY AMANDA PATTON

3

4

Attracting wildlife

Essential for life, water is a magnet for wildlife, but the degree to which birds and beasts will visit your feature depends upon the design. A raised fountain may only attract a passing bird to drink or bathe, but a permanent pond with gently sloping sides or a beach area will draw in a host of creatures, including amphibians, such as frogs and toads, and small mammals. Avoid steep-sided ponds, which pose a hazard to wildlife, as many animals will be unable to escape after being lured into the water.

All water features will turn green eventually when colonised with algae and other organisms, unless the water is moving constantly or circulated through a filter system. Water walls, rills and unplanted features can be chemically treated to prevent discolouration, but in natural ponds, where wildlife and plants would be harmed by chemicals, you can use plants to create a sustainable ecosystem that will minimise algae and weed growth. Oxygenating plants, such as hornwort (*Ceratophyllum demersum*) and water violet (*Hottonia palustris*), are particularly useful, as they mop up the nutrients weeds need to thrive.

3 Cascades create drama and incident and through careful design can be fitted into small, truncated spaces, as well as more generous locations.

DESIGN BY ACRES WILD

4 A pool contained in a large metal bowl makes an incidental feature among low planting. Marginals and dwarf water lilies extend the border into the water.

DESIGN BY IAN KITSON

MAKING A WATER FEATURE

Ponds can be constructed in a variety of ways to suit all pockets. Fibreglass preformed pond liners enable quick installation and come in a wide range of shapes, from formal to naturalistic. Although useful for small features, they can look artificial and be difficult to integrate into a design. Most ponds use butyl rubber liners, which offer a flexible way to create ponds of any size and shape, including bog gardens for moisture-loving plants. The butyl comes in a range of thicknesses and prices.

Shapes for the pond need to be carefully sculpted, with deeper areas for fish and shelves at various levels for baskets of pond plants. Before laying, clear the site of sharp objects that may puncture the liner – the main drawback. Then lay the liner on a bed of soft sand or capillary matting as a cushion. For a natural look use cobbles or gravel over the liner edges to create a seamless union between water and the surrounding garden. Raised water features, such as a brick- or stone-walled tank, are best undertaken by an expert landscaper.

Always consider the safety of a pond – water features are best avoided in gardens used by young children.

Formal pool planted with water lilies by Sarah Massey

PLANTING STYLES

Plants are the living elements that enhance the character of a garden. Over time, signature plants have become associated with particular styles, helping to define the look with their habit, shape, the colour of their flowers and leaves, and seasons of interest. The trick is to marry your garden conditions with a palette of reliable species and varieties that convey the style or theme you want to achieve. Also consider the level of care your chosen plants will require. Designs involving annuals and short-lived perennials, such as cottage gardens, will take more time to maintain than a garden filled with shrubs, so select a style that matches your lifestyle too.

In this section we take a look at a range of planting styles, starting with old favourites 'Cottage to country', and showing how to give these quintessentially English designs a contemporary spin. Designers from Europe and the United States launched the 'Naturalistic style', which mimics nature and includes ornamental grasses and tough perennials. We also consider the Mediterranean garden in this section. Warmer winters and foreign travel have fostered the rise of the urban jungle, the plants for which are outlined in 'Exotic planting'. Its antithesis can be seen in 'Architectural planting', which employs shaped and trained trees and shrubs to create sharply trimmed green rooms. 'Waterside planting' explores the lush interface of the bankside, with planting ideas for the water and surrounding boggy soils. Many gardens include shady zones and 'Shade planting' provides solutions for gloomy areas beside trees or buildings. And finally, the creative use of turf and planting of flower meadows is explored in 'Lawns and meadows'.

LEFT Bold drifts of colourful summer-flowering perennials and ornamental grasses jostle in a naturalistic-style planting in the Hot Garden at RHS Garden Rosemoor in Devon.

DESIGN BY ROGER WEBSTER

BELOW Clipped evergreen trees and low box edging outline and punctuate the framework of this design, providing visual interest when flowers and other ornamentals have faded.

DESIGN BY JAMES SCOTT

Cottage to country

ONE OF THE BEST loved planting designs of the past 100 years, cottage gardens epitomise the romance of British country homesteads of yesteryear, the jewel-like flowers fusing into a confection of colour and form. Country-style planting has similar attributes but with a more formal structure injecting a semblance of order into the design.

Cottage themes

No floral styles historically characterise British gardens more than cottage and country styles. From the joyous jingle-jangle of work-a-day varieties found massed in domestic gardens to the blowsy ebullience of plants in the ample borders that surround many of our historic country houses, these planting styles continue to enthral people across the globe. Both have their roots in history and, over time, have evolved and been embellished to yield ever more sophisticated examples of the garden designers' art.

A hallmark of the modern cottage garden is the mingling of long-flowering annuals and biennials, perennials and seasonal bulbs, naturalised with wild abandon. The approach is casual, with plants encouraged to encroach onto paving, rooting into gaps between slabs or brick paviors or seeding into gravel, and the unexpected effects produced can be enchanting. Depending on space, you can set these beds against a backdrop of small trees or shrubs, such as old-fashioned roses, lilac, flowering currant or crab-apple, with arches and supports swathed in climbers, including clematis and annual sweetpeas. In spring, try daffodils and tulips, together with primulas and aquilegias, and include perennial and annual poppies, foxgloves and *Verbascum* in summer, and asters for autumn interest.

1 A riotous melee of annual and perennial cottage garden plants provides a colourful spectacle.

DESIGN BY CLEVE WEST

2 Fruit trees trained on a rustic stone wall echo the traditions of neighbouring farms.

DESIGN BY CHARLOTTE ROWE

3 Massed tulips provide a spring treat but the bulbs will need replacing every few years.

DESIGN BY CHARLES RUTHERFOORD

4 Cottage garden favourites, such as oriental poppies and salvias, announce the start of the summer season.

DESIGN BY SUE TOWNSEND

Key cottage-style plants

Alchemilla mollis; Apple or crab apple tree varieties, *Alcea rosea* varieties; *Allium schoenoprasum*; *Anemone* species; *Antirrhinum*; *Aquilegia*; *Aster* species; *Leucanthemum* x *superbum*; *Delphinium elatum* varieties; *Digitalis purpurea*; *Galanthus nivalis*; *Gypsophila paniculata, Hesperis matronalis, Linaria purpurea*; *Geranium* species; *Leucanthemum* species; *Lupinus* Russell hybrids; *Nigella damascena*; *Papaver* species, *Primula vulgaris*; *Primula auricula* border varieties; Old-fashioned roses; *Salvia* varieties, Tulip varieties, *Verbascum blattaria*

Digitalis pupurea

Key country-style plants

Achillea filipendulina 'Gold Plate'; *Allium* species; *Anemone hupehensis*; *Artemisia absinthium* 'Lambrook Silver'; *Crambe cordifolia, Campanula lactiflora* and *C. persicifolia* varieties; *Delphinium elatum* species, *Echinacea purpurea* varieties; *Foeniculum vulgaris* 'Purpureum'; *Galega* x *hartlandii* 'Lady Wilson'; *Hydrangea paniculata; Macleaya microcarpa; Mahonia* species; *Miscanthus sinensis* varieties; Herbaceous and tree peony varieties; *Helianthus* varieties; *Phlomis russeliana, Phlox paniculata*; roses, *Salvia nemorosa* and other species; *Stipa gigantea; Verbascum* species; *Viburnum* species

Alliums are country-style stalwarts

1 A broad sweep of lawn and generous flower-filled borders create the ambience of the country garden.

DESIGN BY JAMES SCOTT

2 Bold plantings of Phlomis, blue-green Euphorbia and pinky-red Persicaria.

DESIGN BY SUE TOWNSEND

3 Autumnal plantings meld a red-leaved Cotinus with the flowerheads of grasses, such as Miscanthus and Molinia.

DESIGN BY SUE ADCOCK

4 Pillows of catmint (Nepeta x faassenii) edge a double border of white roses.

DESIGN BY ACRES WILD

Country planting style

To achieve the country style, you ideally need a generous space, with borders not less than 1.8m (6ft) deep to accommodate the massed plantings, although narrower borders that include tall, upright plants and more compact varieties beneath will still produce effective results.

Borders often fringe a central lawn or, if space allows, you can establish a traditional double herbaceous border with a central grass path that creates a feature in itself. While fencing or a wall can provide a backdrop, clipped yew or hornbeam hedges make a wonderful foil for the plantings, as well as providing colour and structure in winter. Borders are usually filled with colour-themed perennials, producing luxuriant symphonies of flower and foliage. But unlike cottage-style schemes where plants are loosely intermingled, those in country gardens are set out in groups or drifts, progressing from the tallest at the back to the smallest in front. However, some tall, slim plants may be used near the front to provide spire-like effects.

Perennial schemes can lack visual interest in winter, so include plants with stout dried stems and seedheads, as well as evergreens and ornamental grasses, which are beautiful at this time of year, particularly in frosty weather. Woody plants give more permanent structure, with species and wild roses, hydrangeas, *Mahonia* and *Viburnum* all providing colour and form throughout the year.

> *"Flowering plants typify the country style, but the blooms can be fleeting. Maintain interest throughout spring and late summer with plants that add structural or textural foliage, such as euphorbias, ferns,* Phlomis russeliana, *and* Artemisia *'Powis Castle'. Try to imagine your beds in black and white and check that they are still interesting."*
>
> JAMES SCOTT

CULTIVATION NOTES

Although seemingly carefree, cottage gardens require careful management to maintain the look. Most of the plants grow best in full sun or semi-shade and in free-draining but moist soil. The soil also needs to be fairly rich; improve it by forking in well-rotted compost or manure in autumn or spring, which will encourage plants to fill out. Although annual and biennial plants are encouraged to self-seed into gaps, the resultant seedlings need to be thinned to allow those remaining to develop – thinned seedlings can be transplanted to fill other areas. To prevent rampant self-seeding remove some flowerheads as they fade. Exhausted perennials should be lifted and divided every few years or replaced to maintain the vigour of the plantings.

Country garden plants require similar care to cottage types. Also prune shrubs and woody plants to keep them in shape, and mulch beds annually with compost to help maintain moisture levels, improve soil fertility and minimise weed growth.

1 Erect spires of Salvia nemorosa 'Caradonna' provide a textural contrast with the long-lasting silky flowerheads of the Mexican feather grass, Stipa tenuissima.

DESIGN BY ACRES WILD

2 The clean architectural lines of a stone seat and raised planter offer a counterpoint to a medley of ornamental grasses and sedges, enlivened by pointillistic bursts of colour from Echinacea and Achillea.

DESIGN BY LOUISE HARRISON-HOLLAND

3 Late summer combinations of blue-flowered asters, Perovskia and Verbena bonariensis.

DESIGN BY CATHERINE HEATHERINGTON

4 Drifts of colourful Helenium and Geranium enliven a border.

DESIGN BY FIONA STEPHENSON

5 Naturalistic-style planting is injected into a formal rose garden with Miscanthus and Molinia grasses.

DESIGN BY WILSON MCWILLIAM

Naturalistic planting

ECHOING THE PRAIRIES of the American Midwest, flower meadows in Britain and Mediterranean scrublands, naturalistic planting looks to nature for inspiration. Plants are massed together to form cushions of colour and texture, and although this style is often used in large gardens, it can be evolved to work in smaller spaces too.

Mirroring nature

The last decade has seen a revolution in garden styles, one of the most significant being the trend in naturalistic planting. By this we mean ornamental plants designed to emulate natural plant communities, with the use of repeated drifts of herbaceous and evergreen perennials and smaller ground-cover plants, together with shrubs and sometimes trees on larger sites. The habitats evoked include grassy British meadowland, American prairie, shrubby Mediterranean garrigue and maquis, and South African fynbos.

Techniques involve the use of perennials with tough constitutions that are able to withstand heavy rain, wind or drought without collapsing or requiring support. Plants are also chosen to best survive the prevailing environmental and soil conditions without the use of fertilisers or

> *"For naturalistic planting with grasses, transparency is a key consideration, allowing other flowering species to be glimpsed through them. Try* Deschampsia cespitosa *'Goldtau',* Molinia *'Heidebraut', and* Calamagrostis x acutiflora *'Karl Foerster', which remains tall and vertical well into the winter months."*
> ANDREW WILSON

maintenance, such as staking. Many also have single blooms that resemble wild plants, with the mass effect, rather than individual floral perfection, the primary visual objective. In addition, single, open flowers provide valuable sources of food for wildlife, such as bees, butterflies and other insects, while the minimal use of fertilisers and intensive horticultural practices also makes naturalistic planting more sustainable and easier to maintain.

Natural planting choices

Instead of planting in rows or small groups, as you would in a flowerbed, the plants in naturalistic schemes are set out in drifts of contrasting colours, forms and textures, with paths weaving among the flowers and foliage. Planting can be colour themed or a riotous assembly of tones, but the palette is normally limited to just a few species, which are then repeated throughout the scheme.

Plants must be robust and able to fend for themselves without pampering, but not so aggressive that they swamp their neighbours. Also select long-flowering varieties that provide a succession of colour and interest throughout the year. Try the early flowering perennials *Helleborus argutifolius*, *Euphorbia characias*, *Geum* and hardy geraniums, underplanted with alliums that will tower over them as they emerge in late spring. In summer, hardy *Salvia*, *Crocosmia*, *Helenium*, *Echinacea* and *Achillea* are all good options, with the larger varieties of *Kniphofia*, *Eryngium*, *Rudbeckia* and *Veronicastrum* providing accents. In autumn, asters continue the display, with dying stems of earlier flowering forms also providing interest.

Grasses are an important ingredient in naturalistic schemes. Mirroring the landscapes of the American prairies, some designers use a mix of grasses to produce ethereal effects, while others balance grasses with flowering perennials to create schemes of a more colourful character. Upright grasses, such as *Calamagrostis* x *acutiflora* 'Karl Foerster', *Miscanthus sinensis*, *Molinia* and *Stipa* are useful in naturalistic schemes; their leaves and flowers ripple in the breeze, giving motion and drama to designs, while the seedheads last throughout autumn and into winter, at the end of which all the plants are cut back.

"Many naturalistic borders peak in late summer and benefit from a planted backdrop of shrubs and climbers that add shape, colour and often fragrance earlier in the season, such as Philadelphus *'Belle Etoile',* Syringa meyeri *'Palibin',* Elaeagnus *'Quicksilver',* Rosa glauca, *honeysuckle and the viticella clematis."*

HELEN ELKS-SMITH

1 Long-flowering yellow Achillea add focal points to this grass-rich design.

DESIGN BY JILL FENWICK

2 The button-like flowers of Allium sphaerocephalon and Verbena bonariensis hover over grassy stems.

DESIGN BY HELEN ELKS-SMITH

3 An informal pathway edged with aromatic herbs meanders through a landscape of contrasting grasses.

DESIGN BY ACRES WILD

4 Drifts of scarlet bergamot, yellow Achillea, orange-red Helenium and lemon Kniphofia fuse in high summer.

DESIGN BY ROGER WEBSTER

5 Pale blue salvias and grasses mingle with peach-pink daylilies, orange Kniphofia and white Achillea.

DESIGN BY AMANDA PATTON

1 Silvery Artemisia creates a dazzling foil for cream Achillea, pink valerian and purple alliums.

DESIGN BY CLEVE WEST

2 Aromatic low-growing herbs intermingle over pale cobbles in this Mediterranean-style garden.

DESIGN BY ACRES WILD

3 A parade of Cordyline and silvery Elaeagnus adds a Mediterranean note to this patio.

DESIGN BY HELEN ELKS-SMITH

4 Cocktails of aromas are released when brushing by the herbs in this sun-soaked garden.

DESIGN BY JAMES BASSON

Mediterranean inspirations

Plants from Mediterranean climates offer solutions for locations that periodically suffer droughts and relatively mild winters. Many herbs, including sage, lavender and rosemary, hail from the Mediterranean, and make colourful contributions to naturalistic planting schemes. Good choices include purple and variegated sage and the various forms of French lavender, *Lavandula stoechas*, as well as silver-leaved shrubs, like *Cistus* and *Helichrysum*. Most Mediterranean species need full sun and free-draining soil to thrive, and will suffer in cold, wet winters, which cause their roots to rot. However, towns and cities in damp regions can provide perfect settings, if the plants are grown in gravel or raised beds filled with sandy soil.

Key naturalistic plants

Achillea millefolium and *A. filipendulina* varieties; *Agastache rugosa* varieties; *Allium sphaerocephalon*; *Anemanthele lessoniana*; *Angelica gigas*; *Astrantia* 'Roma'; *Deschampsia cespitosa* 'Goldtau'; *Eryngium yuccifolium* and *E.* x *zabellii*; *Echinacea purpurea* varieties; *Helenium autumnale* varieties; *Inula magnifica*; *Knautia macedonica*; *Molinia caerulea* 'Edith Dudszus' and *M. c.* 'Transparent'; *Panicum virgatum* varieties; *Pennisetum orientale* 'Tall Tails'; *Persicaria amplexicaule* 'Fire Tails'; *Rudbeckia fulgida*; *Salvia nemorosa* varieties; *Sanguisorba officinalis* 'Red Thunder'; *Sedum telephium* 'Matrona'; *Sporobolus heterolepis*; *Stipa gigantea* and *S. tenuissima*; *Verbascum* species, *Veronicastrum virginicum* 'Fascination'

Echinacea pupurea

5 Echoes of sunnier climes and memories of holidays past are recreated in this dry garden in the country. Cushions of Erigeron karvinskianus draw the eye to an olive tree, which has pride of place.

DESIGN BY SUE TOWNSEND

Exotic planting

BOLD FOLIAGE and bright flowers are the signature ingredients of an exotic or tropical planting style, but while the traditional plants used to evoke this look were tender treasures unable to withstand cold winters, new forms are making it more manageable in cool climes.

Cool tropicals

Wherever we are in the world, many of us like to include plantings that remind us of home or of a memorable holiday or experience. For those living in cool, temperate climates, such as Western Europe, the lure of exotic and tropical-style planting, with dramatic palm trees and large-leaved shrubs, spiced with vibrantly coloured flowers, is a beguiling and increasingly popular proposition. Gardeners in these cooler

ANNUAL INJECTIONS

Bedding dahlias, amaranthus, coleus and gazanias all sport brightly coloured flowers that lend a tropical note to planting schemes, and are easy to grow from seed sown indoors in spring. Sow from March in seed trays or pots of seed compost undercover in a greenhouse or on a windowsill. Transplant the young seedlings and grow on in 7.5cm (3in) pots. Harden off in a cold frame, or set outside during the daytime for a couple of weeks, before planting outdoors after the danger of frost has passed. Purchase bulbs, such as cannas and tender calla lilies, from seed merchants and grow on in pots, planting out as for the annuals above. Alternatively, buy young or semi-mature plants from garden centres.

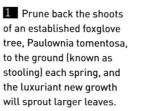

1 Prune back the shoots of an established foxglove tree, Paulownia tomentosa, to the ground (known as stooling) each spring, and the luxuriant new growth will sprout larger leaves.

2 A bold curve of exotic-looking daylilies sweeps past a backdrop of hardy Chusan palms (Trachycarpus) and cabbage palms (Cordyline australis).

DESIGN BY ACRES WILD

3 Hardier bananas, such as Musa basjoo, can survive mild winters in a sheltered spot and, when adequately protected, will reshoot in late spring.

DESIGN BY AMANDA PATTON

4 Hardy bananas, honey-scented Euphorbia mellifera, scarlet-flowered Crocosmia 'Lucifer' and Arbutus x andrachnoides create a luxuriant jungle in a town garden.

DESIGN BY LUCY SOMMERS

5 Large-leaved shrub Tetrapanax papyrifer 'Rex' (far right) sets the right tone among exotic-style perennials such as Persicaria, orange dahlias and vivid crocosmia.

DESIGN BY JULIA FOGG

"A huge spectrum of colours are found in the tropics but when designing at home, try a large dollop of bright orange, red, and hot pink. Kniphofia 'Nobilis', Crocosmia 'Spitfire' and Hemerocallis 'Stafford' are all good hardy candidates. Try these against a green leafy backdrop of bananas (Musa basjoo) and euphorbia."

LUCY SOMMERS

1 Late-flowering red hot poker Kniphofia rooperi makes an imposing display against a screaming scarlet dahlia.

DESIGN BY SUE TOWNSEND

2 Ivy-clad fences, a green-roof and extensive use of bold foliage transform this narrow, shady garden into a lush, leafy retreat.

DESIGN BY CLEVE WEST

Key tropical-style plants

Alstroemeria varieties; *Arundo donax*; *Canna* varieties; *Catalpa bignonioides* 'Aurea'; Dahlia varieties, especially Bishop series; *Dicksonia antarctica*; *Echium pininana*; *Eriobotrya japonica*; *Eucomis bicolor* and *E. comosa*; *Hedychium species* and varieties; *Hemerocallis*, especially large gaudy hybrids; *Fatsia japonica*; *Lobelia tupa*; *Melianthus major*; *Miscanthus sacchariflorus*; *Musa basjoo* and *M.sikkimensis*; *Paulownia tomentosa*; *Phormium* species and varieties; *Phyllostachys* species; *Ricinus communis*; *Tetrapanax papyrifer*; *Trachycarpus fortunei*; *Verbena bonariensis*; *Yucca* species and varieties, *Zantedeschia* species and hybrids

Canna lily

3 A lush, secluded enclave in a shady nook is enhanced through the careful positioning of tree ferns and a textural underplanting of shade plants.
DESIGN BY PATRICIA FOX

4 Pared-down planting in a shady corner radiates cool charm. Tree ferns are underplanted with deciduous Hakonechloa grass and clipped globes of evergreen box.
DESIGN BY TOM STUART-SMITH

shrubs, such as the Indian bean tree *Catalpa bignonioides, Magnolia grandiflora* and *Aralia*, together with the Chusan palm, *Trachycarpus fortunei*, which all have bold foliage that lends itself to this style. Hardy perennials, such as the exotic-looking daylily *Hemerocallis* and *Crocosmia* add floral piquancy in summer, and leafy plants, including hostas, *Fatsia*, and *Farfugium japonicum*, which can be used to create a lush understorey, add an exotic flavour while sailing through cold winters outside.

CULTIVATION NOTES

For gardeners in areas that experience sub-zero temperatures and cold, wet winters, this style will require high levels of maintenance, as many of the plants used must be covered or brought inside over winter. Some tender plants, particularly succulents, will tolerate freezing conditions if their roots are kept dry or if they can regenerate from bulbs and rootstocks below ground.

Tender and exotic plants need good soil conditions, but they range in light requirements, from full sun to shade, depending on species or variety. Cannas and dahlias prefer sun, while begonias and tree ferns, together with other plants hailing from jungle environments, are happiest in shade.

To minimise the risk of losing borderline hardy plants in winter, cover the crowns of tree ferns and palms with insulating material, such as dry straw covered with horticultural fleece. Also mulch plants such as dahlias and hardy bananas with a thick layer of bark chips or other material to protect them from penetrating frosts; remove the mulch once the danger has passed and plants start to regrow in spring. Growing tender plants in pots makes the job of moving them in and out of the greenhouse easier too.

climes can choose from a variety of plants that will express this unfettered lushness. In recent years, introductions from higher altitudes in tropical and sub-tropical regions has resulted in a greater number of plants, including *Tetrapanax papyrifer* 'Rex' and the banana, *Musa basjoo*, that will tolerate lower winter temperatures. A warming climate and the urban heat-island effect of towns and cities, which raises ambient temperatures, has also allowed plants that are normally thought of as tender to thrive in British gardens.

Exotics for all seasons

The exotic planting style reaches a peak during the summer months when tender plants and flowers, including *Canna* and *Dahlia* are in full bloom. Spring colour can be introduced with ferns, such as *Matteuccia struthiopteris*, and *Zantedeschia aethiopica*, while *Hedychium gardnerianum* and *Nerine bowdenii* will contribute late autumn interest, when some of the tenderest plants will already be under cover. To avoid a blank canvas in winter, include some hardy evergreens, such as ferns, and structural trees and

1 The sculptural lines of a mature Japanese maple are exhibited perfectly against a timber deck, creating a exciting focal point.

DESIGN BY NIGEL PHILIPS

2 Erect stems of moisture-loving horsetails (Equisetum camschatense) make architectural walls around a formal pool.

DESIGN BY ANTHONY PAUL

3 A tableau of textural greenery is created with a curtain of bamboo, clipped box and a leafy hydrangea set against natural stone.

DESIGN BY DENISE CADWALLADER

4 Statuesque small trees can be grown in big pots, but must be kept watered and fed regularly.

DESIGN BY ANDREW WILSON

5 Clipped and sculpted evergreen shrubs are useful counterpoints for relaxed plantings of ornamental grasses.

DESIGN BY TOM STUART-SMITH

Architectural planting

SCULPTURAL LEAVES, striking stems and tightly trimmed topiary create the planting architecture within a garden. These bold evergreen and deciduous forms help to mould the design, and can be used to catch the eye, enclose a space, or add drama to wintry landscapes when the flowers of summer are long gone.

Bold ideas

Architectural plantings are dramatic and awe-inspiring. Plants that can be shaped and used to underpin the geometry of a garden have been important designers' tools for many centuries, and the key to success is to use them sparingly and where they will have most impact; what is left out is just as important as what is included.

With a palette of small-leaved evergreen trees and shrubs, you can create architectural structures, such as hedgerows, to construct the building blocks of a garden design, as well as geometrical or abstract sculptural forms to produce distinctive focal points that draw the eye. In fact, many plants possess such versatility they can morph into shapes that would be difficult or expensive to create using any other means. Some styles rely on architectural

"I often include plants that provide texture and colour in winter, such as clipped yew, box and beech, and combine these with handsome grasses, including Calamagrostis *'Karl Foerster',* Hakonechloa macra, *and* Miscanthus *'Starlight', which offer movement and contrast beautifully with the static topiary."*

TOM STUART-SMITH

planting to achieve the look: for example, parterre gardens are made up of *Buxus sempervirens* trained into intricate patterns on beds of gravel, while contemporary architectural style employs closely clipped hedges to enforce the rigour of geometry on the design. In addition, boundaries in all types of garden are often defined with yew, beech or hornbeam hedges to convey the illusion of an outdoor room, and to control the vistas within the space and of the landscape beyond.

Ornamental plants are included in architectural schemes in varying degrees. Some designers eschew the use of flowering plants altogether, relying on architectural foliage plants and hard landscaping to carry the scheme. Others deploy blooms in tightly controlled ways to create bursts of colour, or they may use single colour themes, with white or pale yellow perennials, seasonal bulbs or bedding plants to reinforce the cool calmness of the space.

Clipped forms

Plants that can withstand continual and close clipping and regenerate from dormant buds when hard pruned are ideal for hedging and topiary. Box (*Buxus sempervirens*) is a dense-foliaged evergreen shrub frequently used for low to medium-sized hedges, while dark evergreen yew

1 The interplay of clipped and architectural forms of evergreen and deciduous trees and shrubs provides a feast of contrasting shapes and textures.

DESIGN BY CHARLOTTE ROWE

2 A regiment of standard hornbeams (Carpinus betulus), clipped into cubes on plinths of evergreen box conveys a sense of formality and order.

DESIGN BY CAROLINE DAVY

3 Clipped forms provide important structure in winter when the cacophony of summer has vanished.

DESIGN BY ROSEMARY ALEXANDER

4 A large conifer is transformed by cloud-pruning, its globular shapes emphasised by spheres of box below.

DESIGN BY NIGEL PHILIPS

Key plants for architectural planting

Amelanchier x *lamarckii*; *Buxus sempervirens*; *Carpinus betulus*; *Cornus* species; *Euonymus japonicus*; *Fagus sylvatica*; *Ilex aquifolium* and *I. crenata*; *Laurus nobilis*; *Lonicera nitida*; *Ligustrum* species; *Picea glauca* var *albertiana* 'Conica'; *Thuja occidentalis* 'Smaragd'; *Pinus* species; *Prunus laurocerasus* and *P. lusitanica*; *Rhododendron* species; *Taxus baccata*; *Viburnum* species

Cloud-pruned Ilex crenata

(*Taxus baccata*) is suitable for taller hedges and creates a wonderful foil for statuary or decorative planting. Both box and yew are also ideal for topiary forms. Deciduous trees, such as hornbeam (*Carpinus betulus*), and beech (*Fagus sylvatica*), make effective hedgerows for architectural schemes, their ridged green foliage and dead bronze leaves, which are retained in winter, providing colour and texture all year round. Their winter coats contrast beautifully with evergreen conifers, too.

Punctuation marks

Designers also use a wide spectrum of woody plants with architectural forms to punctuate their schemes. Many trees and shrubs have naturally imposing shapes that can be used to complement architectural designs, either as single focal points, or as punctuation throughout the design. Examples include hollies, *Amelanchier*, *Viburnum rhytidophyllum* and *Carpinus betulus* 'Fastigiata' – their shapes embellished through clipping, thinning or raising the crown to reveal the stems beneath. Some shrubs, such as *Ilex crenata*, can be cloud-pruned, where the canopy is clipped into globes to create striking features, often seen in Asian gardens and now popular in the west. Spheres of box, either single specimens or grouped like giant green marbles, are also highly effective in contemporary designs.

Waterside planting

THRIVING IN DAMP soil or paddling at the edges of a pool, waterside planting lends a colourful fringe around features and invites an abundance of wildlife to the party too. Water lilies and other aquatics add to the drama, their exquisite flowers decorating the glassy surface.

Plants for pools and ponds

One of the most exciting elements in a garden, water is frequently used in isolation to create drama and atmosphere, but features that also include aquatic and bankside plantings have a character all their own. Lush, exuberant idylls, they conjure a sense of surprise in a garden, like stumbling on a desert oasis. The diversity of plants available is as astonishing and rich as for any other aspect of the garden, with plants to suit every style, from large lakes to tiny patio water features. If carefully chosen, aquatics can be used to great effect in formal and geometric designs as well as more naturalistic settings.

If you want to include aquatic planting, design a feature that can accommodate your favourites, with varying water depths and conditions that will suit the different plant groups. Create deep areas for water lilies (*Nymphaea*), whose rootstocks and stems must be submerged, while their leaves and flowers float on the surface. Marginal plants grow on the bankside: some, like the vigorous flag irises (*Iris pseudacorus*), are happy with their roots submerged, others, including *Iris ensata*, prefer to be just below the surface, while a third type, *Iris sibirica,* thrive with their roots just dipped in water or in boggy soil. Floating aquatics, including the water pineapple (*Stratiotes aloides*), live a sedentary life partially submerged or floating on the surface. Moisture-loving perennial plants, including skunk cabbage (*Lysichiton*) and many primulas, are ideal for the boggy areas around a natural pond, where the soil is permanently saturated or wet for much of the year. These bog plants can be grouped to create a lush and leafy fringe around the water's edge.

PLANTING POND PERIMETERS

The design of a pond and type of planting used exerts huge influence over the character of the surrounding garden. A feature with gently sloping sides will allow bog plants and marginals to merge seamlessly from the damp soil on the banks to water up to 45cm (18in) deep, creating a gradual, dream-like transition. A steeper slope or sudden drop will truncate the effect, creating a more definite edge or line.

An artificial pond will not necessarily have boggy margins but you can create a marshy area. Dig a hole at least 60cm (2ft) deep beside your pond and line it with butyl or similar pond liner. Pierce the liner with a few holes, add a layer of grit, and then refill with the excavated soil mixed with well-rotted compost. Water the bog regularly during dry spells.

1 A stream's edging of understated perennials, annual daisies and ferns enhances the naturalistic design.

DESIGN BY FIONA STEPHENSON

2 Successions of aquatic plants positioned on submerged terraces emerge from ever deepening water, fusing the planting design of the pond with the surrounding borders on drier ground.

DESIGN BY IAN KITSON

3 Rich and diverse poolside planting helps anchor a water feature into the landscape and controls the views across the water surface.

DESIGN BY ACRES WILD

4 The angle of the bank and depth of water in a pond will influence the range of plants you can grow, with some large water lilies requiring water one metre (3ft) deep or more to thrive.

DESIGN BY JAMES SCOTT

> *"Reflections are extremely valuable in winter and tall vertical structure is essential. Include reeds and rushes, such as the skeletal deciduous forms of Phragmites australis, or evergreens like Carex morrowii. I also plant Viburnum opulus; its cherry-red berries persist in winter, as birds only feast on them when times are tough."*
>
> THOMAS HOBLYN

1 An enchanting partnership of water irises and flowering rush (Butomus umbellatus).

DESIGN BY ACRES WILD

2 Parasol-leaved Damera peltata and yellow Caltha palustris luxuriate in damp soil.

DESIGN BY ARABELLA LENNOX-BOYD

3 Boldly-detailed steps and exuberant waterside planting herald a dramatic natural pond.

DESIGN BY THOMAS HOBLYN

4 In small ponds, plant in baskets filled with aquatic compost and cover with gravel.

DESIGN BY WILSON MCWILLIAM

Designing with flowers and foliage

The largest group of aquatics are the marginal plants, which offer a wide range of flower colours and forms. Choose a range that flowers at different times to maintain interest, starting in spring with *Caltha and Lysichiton*, and following on in summer with irises, *Lychnis* and water lilies, amongst others, with the rushes, such as *Typha*, providing autumn interest. Bog plants can be used to fill lulls in the pond planting. Although many water plants have outstanding flowers, many have equally beautiful foliage, which can be used to create a variety of effects. For example, an imposing clump of a single species, such as the vividly striped sword-like *Iris pseudacorus* 'Variegata' or parasol-leaved *Darmera peltata,* will provide architectural accents. For a minimalist look, try clumps of a single variety of Japanese water iris *(Iris ensata)*, or mix complementary flower types to create a slight variation in tone, but parity in leaf form. Moisture-loving plants also lend a luxuriance that may not be present in other parts of the garden. Giant-leafed perennial colossi, such as the Chilean rhubarb *(Gunnera manicata)* and ornamental rhubarb *(Rheum palmatum)* love moist soil, and produce leaves that are often an arm-span or more across.

CULTIVATION NOTES

When designing your pond, include shelves around the edges to accommodate marginal plants and a deeper area in the centre for aquatics, such as water lilies. For details on how to construct a pond, see p.87.

It is best to fill your water feature with rainwater, rather than from the mains, as it is better for wildlife and the ecological balance in the pond. Levels will need to be maintained during the summer, using water from a butt if possible during dry spells or adding mains water gradually so that it does not change the temperature too rapidly.

You can either create a planting bed at the bottom of the pond with a layer of garden soil, or contain your plants in pond baskets filled with garden soil or aquatic compost – do not use potting composts as they are too rich in nutrients and will encourage weeds. A mulch of gravel will help to keep the soil or compost in place. If you did not create the pond yourself and it does not include shelves or shallow areas, you can still include marginals by planting them in baskets and propping them up on bricks. Include oxygenating plants, such as *Ceratophyllum demersum*, checking that those you plan to use are not invasive species and causing problems in the wild, some of which are still available to buy. Most aquatic plants need to be lifted and divided every few years to rejuvenate them and maintain flowering.

Waterside plants

BOG PLANTS: *Astilbe* species; *Darmera peltata; Eupatorium cannabinum; Gunnera manicata; Iris sibirica* varieties; *Osmunda regalis; Primula pulverulenta; Primula florindae; Rodgersia* species; *Rheum palmatum*
MARGINALS AND AQUATICS: *Caltha palustris; Iris ensata* varieties; *Iris pseudacorus* 'Variegata'; *Lobelia cardinalis; Lychnis flos-cuculi; Lysichiton americanus* and *L. camtschatcensis; Nymphaea* varieties; *Orontium aquaticum; Schoenoplectus tabernaemontani* 'Zebrinus'; *Typha latifolia* 'Variegata', *Typha minima; Zantedeschia aethiopica* 'Crowborough' and other varieties

Iris sibirica

Shade planting

COOL LEAFY landscapes have a charm all of their own, combining deciduous trees' seasonal show of blossom, foliage, fruit and stem, with continuous colour from evergreens, while dainty woodland flowers lend decorative highlights beneath the canopies.

Cool environments

Most, if not all, gardens have areas in shade, or at least where light is significantly diminished for part of the day. Cast by trees and hedges, or buildings and other structures such as fences in urban areas, shade imposes a unique set of circumstances that many plants favour, and these valuable species can be harnessed to enliven gloomy spaces in the garden.

Shade-tolerate plants usually inhabit woodlands in the wild. Some are deciduous, growing and flowering in spring before the tree leaves unfurl and then dying down; others are evergreen and just sit out the low light conditions by growing slowly. Those that have adapted to live under or very close to the trees are also tolerant of drought, competing with the larger plants' roots, while the leafy canopies above them act like umbrellas, shielding them

> *"Spring-flowering perennials make colourful partners for bulbs in shady borders. Choose the reliable pink* Geranium macrorrhizum; *Brunnera 'Jack Frost', with its icy green leaves and clear blue flowers; the orchid-like blooms of* Epimedium x versicolor 'Sulphureum', *which appear ahead of new foliage; and aquilegias."*
>
> ANDREW FISHER TOMLIN

1 Simple planting of white-stemmed birch and shade-tolerant ferns bring this tiny timber-decked courtyard to life.

DESIGN BY STUART CRAINE

2 A slate seat enclave shaded by surrounding birch trees is enlivened by a wide range of spring-flowering plants, including dainty Epimedium and pink-flowered Bergenia and Lamprocapnos, while the unfurling fronds of Dryopteris ferns add fresh appeal.

DESIGN BY ANDREW FISHER TOMLIN

3 Shade-tolerant plants, such as bronze-leaved Heuchera and Bergenia with its round foliage, clothe a shady green wall installation and continue into the garden below.

DESIGN BY PATRICIA FOX

4 The canopies of a number of hardy evergreen trees and shrubs have coalesced to create a sheltered, shady retreat in this narrow town garden.
DESIGN BY CLEVE WEST

5 An elegant, but shady, façade is made more imposing by the careful positioning of two clipped standard laurels underplanted with a froth of variegated ivy.
DESIGN BY JOHN BROOKES

CLIMBING HIGH

Many climbing plants for shade are as attractive as their sun-loving relatives. Some are self-supporting, using stem roots to adhere to walls or fences. These include the ivies, the climbing hydrangea, *Hydrangea petiolaris*, and its close relative *Schizophragma integrifolium*. Others, such as *Parthenocissus henryana*, with its decorative divided foliage, stick with suckers. Shade-tolerant twiners will need support, and include honeysuckles, such as *Lonicera* x *tellmanniana* and *L. henryi*, spring-flowering *Clematis alpina* and *C. macropetala*, as well as some large-flowered forms, such as pink-striped *Clematis* 'Nelly Moser', white 'Marie Boisselot' and purple-red 'Warsaw Nike'.

1 A shady terrace becomes a leafy jungle with potted tree ferns of various heights and a range of shade-tolerant perennials.

DESIGN BY DENISE CADWALLADER

2 The lower leaves of black bamboo (Phyllostachys nigra) have been removed to reveal its glossy stems.

DESIGN BY DAN PEARSON

3 This moist, shady border behind a tall wall has been transformed with Japanese maples, ferns and rhododendrons.

DESIGN BY JAMES SCOTT

4 Urban gardens often have shady spots created by adjacent buildings, offering space for leafy woodland plants.

DESIGN BY CATHERINE HEATHERINGTON

5 Moist shady areas around tall buildings make ideal homes for a range of textural plants, such as sedges and hostas.

DESIGN BY MERILEN MENTAAL

6 Before the leaf canopies of trees reduce light levels, naturalised bulbs such as daffodils provide colourful displays.

DESIGN BY ARABELLA LENNOX-BOYD

Shade-tolerant plants

Alchemilla mollis; Anemone x hybrida; Arundinaria murielae; Astilbe species and varieties; *Athyrium* varieties; *Aucuba japonica* and varieties; *Bergenia* varieties; *Brunnera macrophylla* varieties; *Buxus sempervirens; Camellia japonica* and *C.* x *williamsii; Daphne laureola; Dicentra* species; *Digitalis purpurea* varieties; *Dryopteris* species; *Helleborus x hybridus* varieties; *Epimedium* species; *Fatsia japonica; Galanthus nivalis; Geranium phaeum* varieties; *Heuchera* and *heucherella* varieties; *Hosta* species; *Hydrangea* species; *Hypericum androsaemum* and *H. calycinum; Lamium maculatum* varieties; *Lamprocapnos spectabilis; Luzula nivea; Mahonia japonica* and *M.* x *media; Phyllostachys aurea* and *P. nigra; Pulmonaria* species and varieties; *Rhododendron* species and hybrids; *Rubus odoratus; Sarcococca* species; *Tiarella* species and varieties; *Tricyrtis* species and varieties; *Viburnum* species; *Vinca minor*

Camellia japonica

CULTIVATION NOTES

Check plant labels to ensure you are growing your chosen plants in the optimum amount of light for those particular species, as some will only tolerate light shade. Soil moisture requirements also vary depending on the plant, and plants, such as rhododendrons and camellias, require acid soil. You can include moisture-loving plants under trees if you install raised beds filled with good quality garden soil, but remember to water them during prolonged periods of drought. Also improve soils with an annual mulch of home-made leaf mould, made by composting autumn leaves in a strong plastic bag, tied at the top and punctured with holes, then left to rot down for a year or two. Alternatively, mulch with well-rotted compost or manure.

from rain. Other shade-loving plants grow at the woodland edges, just beyond the tree canopies where the soil is moist and enriched with leaf litter.

Plants for woodland glades

The subdued light and moist soil at the woodland edge provide optimum conditions for the widest range of plants. For designers, this is an important ecological niche, presenting the greatest potential for exciting combinations and plant breeders have now developed a range of colourful shrubs, climbers, herbaceous perennials and bulbs that will light up even the darkest areas.

Many shade-loving plants are low growing perennials, which form clumps or creep through the soil via stems above or below ground. Useful for carpeting areas beneath trees and shrubs, they include dead nettle (*Lamium*), male ferns (*Dryopteris filix-mas*), *Vinca minor, Geranium phaeum* and *Sarcococca humilis,* and form a thick layer of weed-suppressing leaves. Many plants that thrive in shade have bold, shapely foliage, which may be variegated or, occasionally, silvery. Examples include *Astelia, Heuchera, Aucuba* and *Pulmonaria*, although few plants with colourful leaves tolerate very dark sites.

Many woodland plants flower in spring, and often sport white or pale petals or perfumed blooms that can be located easily in the darkness by pollinating insects. These include the shrubs *Camellia, Rhododendron* and *Pieris*, as well as bulbs, such as daffodils, snowdrops, hardy cyclamen and bluebells. In summer, hydrangeas, *Geranium phaeum* varieties, *Anemone* x *hybrida* and others, pick up the baton when the spring-flowering shrubs and bulbs start to lose their lustre. A few plants, including the scented *Mahonia* x *media* and Christmas box (*Sarcoccoca*), exploit the winter months, producing blooms when there is little competition for light and filling the cold air with delicious perfume.

1 The linear carpet of pavior-edged turf and architectural lines of the pleached hedge above combine to produce a play on perspective, making the garden appear longer.

DESIGN BY ACRES WILD

2 Amoebic expanses of turf covering a variety of slopes and levels provides visual continuity from above, but plays with the visitor's perception at ground level.

DESIGN BY IAN KITSON

3 Close-mown turf can be seen as a living canvas. These giant paviors inlaid into the grass produce a dynamic pattern as they march across the landscape.

DESIGN BY CHRIS ZBROZYNA

4 Lawns located on two levels are linked by a carpet of Festuca gautieri, a drought-tolerant grass suitable for areas of light traffic.

DESIGN BY MERILEN MENTAAL

5 Bold stripes generated by cutting the grass with a cylinder mower accentuate the lay of the land and create texture and colour that adds interest to large expanses of lawn.

DESIGN BY JAMES SCOTT

6 The central turf pathway that conjoins two sumptuous mixed borders at the Sir Harold Hillier Gardens and Arboretum is obliquely intersected by pathways that allow visits to explore the plants on either side.

DESIGN BY JULIA FOGG

Lawns and meadows

SOFT AND LUSH, a lawn fulfils many functions, providing a green foil for planting, a play surface for games, and an inexpensive yet flexible landscaping material that suits almost any garden style. With a little imagination, turf and other low-growing plants can also be used in a myriad of ways to enhance your design.

Designing with grass

The green baize of a meticulously manicured lawn is the quintessential feature of an English garden. Whether a visual respite from a riotous cottage border or a textural foil for a crisp contemporary garden, the lawn is much more than a space on which to walk or play. But lawns are so commonplace, their contribution to the success of a garden is often overlooked, yet in the hands of a skilled designer this flexible medium serves many purposes. It can link disparate spaces, galvanising them into a cohesive whole, and when cut into geometric shapes, particularly circles, lawns act as focal points, drawing the eye to the centre of the garden and helping to disguise awkwardly shaped plots. A simple mantle of mown turf over contoured ground will bestow dynamic rhythm, while long grass studded with

"Think about grass as an aesthetic – a visual texture rather than just a utilitarian surface. It's easy to experiment by weaving mown grass with informal bands of longer grass, where bulbs and perennials can offer seasonal highlights, as it's a fast-growing material and any mistakes are quickly rectified."

JULIA FOGG

1 Synthetic turf is often a viable proposition where conditions are unsuitable for turf, such as play areas or gardens in deep shade.

DESIGN BY JANINE PATTISON

2 Instead of close-mowing all the turf allow some areas to grow longer to add visual diversity. Sowing wild flower seeds or naturalising bulbs and perennials will add further interest through the seasons.

DESIGN BY HELEN ELKS-SMITH

CULTIVATION NOTES

To keep turf in good condition it needs regular maintenance, including weekly mowing, and feeding and aerating in spring and autumn. Good light and moisture are required for strong grass growth, although established lawns can endure periodic drought – they may turn brown, but will quickly recover when rain returns – and irrigation in most instances is not needed. Even so, you may want to install underground irrigation systems and pop-up sprinklers before the turf is laid, just in case. Computer controlled timers help regulate the more efficient use of water.

Although turf will survive in semi-shade, it deteriorates in dense shade, particularly in heavily used areas. Special mixes for shady areas are available, but even these will not be able to sustain heavy wear. Layers of wet autumn leaves that sit on the grass for any length of time after falling will also rob the grass of light and air and cause it to deteriorate.

Compaction, caused by constant use, has a deleterious effect on turf and may eventually kill the grass, so consider the routes around the garden, and select alternative landscaping materials, such as paving, gravel, or bricks set into the turf, for main pathways.

Dogs, particularly bitches, can also cause problems; their urine scorches the turf and causes unsightly yellow patches. Products are now available to put into dogs' feed to minimise discolouration.

wild flowers or naturalised bulbs emulates agricultural landscapes or parkland of yesteryear, while also providing a habitat for insects, such as bees, butterflies and moths.

Although most people remove turf to create beds, you could create an historic feature, such as a 'parterre de broderie', where turf is cut into intricate patterns, with the gaps infilled with colourful stones or gravel. Mazes and labyrinths, loved by children and adults, are other options. Formed by a sinuous network of grass paths, they make unusual and dynamic features for larger gardens.

Mowing effects

Classic lawn stripes, created using a cylinder mower with a rear roller, can produce a powerfully decorative, albeit temporary feature. If the mower follows the contour of the land, the dramatic sweep of lines will further accentuate a vista, while a simple striped rectangular lawn can smarten up a formal design. Altering the height of cut adds a further creative dimension, with longer grass delivering a more natural look. Leaving the grass longer has the added benefit of reducing mowing frequency, too, and allows you to include naturalised spring bulbs and other wild flowers and perennials into the mix.

Grasses for lawns

Turf is a mix of various creeping grasses blended to form a hard-wearing carpet of leaves or 'sward'. It can be sown from seed or created by laying turf on a prepared surface.

Plants for naturalising in grass

BULBS FOR SHORT GRASS: *Anemone nemorosa,
Chionodoxa lucilae, Crocus tommasinianus,
C. chrysanthus, Erythronium dens-canis; Fritillaria
meleagris, Galanthus nivalis; Iris reticulata; Narcissus
bulbocodium, N.cyclamineus, N. 'February Gold',
N. obvallaris; Ornithogalum nutans; Scilla siberica*
PLANTS FOR LONGER GRASS: *Camassia; Campanula
latiloba; Centaurea macrocephala; Crambe cordifolia;
Euphorbia griffithii; E. palustris; Galtonia candicans;
Geranium
psilostemon;
Gladiolus communis;
Lathyrus latifolius;
Leucanthemum
vulgare; Narcissus
species*

Fritillaria meleagris

Most designers use turf for an instant effect, as it establishes
quickly, but seed offers a wider choice of grass varieties,
including species that suit specific environments, such as
shade, or grasses mixed with wild flowers.

For a lawn that is used only occasionally or for
ornamental purposes only, try low growing species, such
as *Festuca gautieri*, and other drought-tolerant fescues.
Other groundcover plants suitable for occasional traffic
include thyme, chamomile, sedum, *Crassula* and *Soleirolia
soleirolii*. Play surfaces need tougher species, such as
perennial ryegrass and smooth-stalked meadow grass.

In hot climates where prolonged drought is a threat,
Bermuda grass (*Cynodon dactylon*), buffalo grass (*Buchloe
dactyloides*), and *Paspalum* species are used as single
species rather than a mix to avoid a patchy effect.

Consider alternative surfaces, including synthetic turf,
in recreational areas, particularly around play equipment,
which have high foot traffic. The appearance and durability
of turfing fabrics has improved considerably in the last few
years and from a distance they are difficult to distinguish
from the real thing.

CREATING MEADOWS

Meadows are composed of largely self-sustaining
herbaceous flowering plants and native grasses. Your
choice of plants will be dictated by the nutrient content
and type of soil in your garden, and the amount of
moisture available. Choose from the wide ranges of
seed mixtures on offer, which include different blends
of wild flowers, some mixed with grasses, designed to
produce a range of floristic effects on a variety of soils.

The best meadows are created on impoverished
soils where nutrients, such as nitrogen and phosphorus,
are in short supply. This keeps vigorous grasses in
check, allowing the wild flowers space to grow and
flower. One trick to reduce fertility is to invert the soil
profile and expose the subsoil, which is comparatively
impoverished, or import subsoil from elsewhere. It is
also important to cut the plants at the right times to
guarantee success. Mow meadows in summer after
they have flowered and sown their seed for future
generations, and then again in autumn to help control
the grasses. After each cut, remove the clippings which,
if left in place, will fertilise the soil and shade out the
plants beneath.

If creating a meadow in a small area, choose ox-eye
daisies (*Leucanthemum vulgare*), buttercups (*Ranunculus
acris*) and yellow rattle (*Rhinanthus minor*), and plant
bulbs, such as daffodils (*Narcissus*), camassias and
snakeshead fritillaries (*Fritillaria meleagris*), which can
be left to naturalise.

Meadow planting in a modern garden by Mandy Buckland

OUTDOOR EXPERIENCES

Relaxing

KEY INGREDIENTS in any garden, furniture, heaters and cooking facilities allow you to relax, socialise and entertain, while also contributing to the garden's style.

CHOOSING SEATING

Whether choosing a dining set, incidental seat, sofa, hanging chair or hammock, shop around for a design that is fit for purpose and makes a statement, just like a piece of sculpture, and suits the character of your garden. Many can be bought from garden centres, but also look online or consider commissioning a craftsman to make a bespoke item. Period and rustic furniture can be sourced from architectural salvage outlets and auctions. Also consider the pros and cons of seating materials, which include:

- Timber: choose from softwood or hardwood; softwood needs preservatives to prevent decay, hardwood is more durable. Timber can be painted any colour. Always choose sustainably sourced products *(see p.143)*.
- Wicker: traditionally woven from natural cane, which decays quickly unless preserved or painted; man-made alternatives are more durable. Both are very light.
- Precast aluminium: light and easily moulded, it is often used for furniture frames. Seats can be uncomfortable.
- Fabrics: available in vast range of colours and patterns, ensure materials are weather-resistant or bring indoors in winter. Marine-grade leather is comfortable, but needs treating to keep supple.
- Plastics: easily moulded or woven, lightweight, and available in many textures and colours. Check plastics are UV stabilised, and look for furniture made from recycled materials for an eco-friendly option.

"To create a sense of unity, use the same materials and style for built-in seating as you've chosen for features elsewhere in the garden. And for comfort, ensure the seat depth is between 40 and 45cm (15–18in)."
AMANDA PATTON

FREE-STANDING SEATING

Furniture that can be independently moved and arranged is known as free standing and includes chairs, tables, sofas, stools and swing chairs supported on frameworks. This type of seating is easy to integrate into a design, but ensure your patio or area of hard standing is large enough to fit your chosen furniture and that it suits the style of your garden.

Free-standing seats: points to consider

- Choose a design sympathetic in size and scale to the space available, and allow for seats to be moved out from under a dining table.
- Seats should be light enough to be moved around easily unless you are opting for sofas that won't be moved.
- Select materials for their longevity, durability and graceful ageing.
- Ensure seats are comfortable when used for long periods; use cushions on hard metal and timber seats.
- Check foldaway items are easily dismantled for storage, along with cushions and other soft furnishings.
- Ensure seats don't collect water, accelerating decay.

FIXED SEATING

Seats constructed as an integral part of the design can make exciting design features, and include wide copings on raised beds or pond edges that double as seats, and benches with useful storage areas beneath.

Fixed seating: points to consider

- Choose the position and site carefully; seats in full sun, deep shade or a wind tunnel will limit their comfort.
- Fixed seating is often more appropriate for incidental or casual use, rather than longer periods of relaxation.
- As constructed items, seats are best installed by professional contractors to guarantee safety.
- The materials and design style needs careful consideration before inclusion in a scheme.
- Bespoke fixed seating set at strategic points can allow individuals with infirmities to enjoy more of the garden.

WINTER PROTECTION

Many types of garden furniture require some protection over winter. Check the durability of the materials before you make your purchases and establish the nature of any guarantee. Cushions and soft furnishings need dry, airy storage facilities either indoors or in a shed or sealed unit outside over winter. Plastic covers afford protection from rain and frost for wood and metal furniture.

1 The clean lines of a modern suite sit comfortably in this contemporary elevated space; the design is enlivened by chequered cushions that add just the right level of contrast.

2 If your furniture will remain outdoors all year round, ensure it is made from materials that are weatherproof and will not fade or deteriorate in strong sunlight, such as this sofa in marine-grade faux leather.

3 Fixed seating can make an important visual statement in a garden and needs to be planned into the design process.

DESIGN BY AMANDA PATTON

4 When used as a focal point or incidental feature, furniture makes a powerful statement. Select the design and colour to help establish the style characteristic of the space.

DESIGN BY CHRIS GUTTERIDGE

CREATING SHADE

Although shade may be cast by adjacent buildings, trees or structures, additional shielding from strong sunlight may be required. Instant and permanent shade can be created by roofed structures, such as an atrium, summerhouse or arbour, or use pergolas with slatted roofs to produce dappled shade. Fabric supported on structures, such as a gazebo over a dining or sitting area, affords temporary shade, or you could use a sail slung between uprights, which can be quickly dismantled in gusty conditions. Umbrellas or parasols are flexible options; those with adjustable arms attached to weighted bases are ideal for outdoor lounges and dining rooms. Check that canopies can be adjusted to provide shade where it's needed and have ratchet systems to aid opening. Also ensure they are sturdy and are not blown inside out easily. Although most canopies can be left outside, they are best kept under cover in winter.

Shading: points to consider

- Assess whether you require permanent or temporary shading solutions, and the density of cover needed.
- Use of fixed architectural features to create shade needs to be factored into the initial design process.
- Any temporary shading system should be fit for purpose and enhance the ambience of the garden.
- Select umbrellas and parasols that are weather resistant and fully adjustable.
- Ensure you have sufficient facilities for winter storage.

HEATING SOLUTIONS

Relaxing and socialising in the garden is dependent not only on the comfort of your furniture but also the outdoor temperature. Night temperatures can dramatically contrast with day after sunset, particularly in early and late summer, and supplementary heating can be used to increase your enjoyment of the garden over a longer period, temporarily warming areas to make them more comfortable while also providing atmospheric lighting.

Fixed fires act as dramatic focal points, but consider the effects on the environment when choosing designs and fuel types, as some are more energy efficient than others, and use heating units sparingly. Solid fuels should be smokeless and always ensure open fires and naked flames are kept away from children, pets and flammable features. Always buy from reputable suppliers and follow safety instructions.

1 Shade can be created with movable canopies and parasols, or permanent structures such as pergolas, the degree of cover determined by the number of slats or use of climbing plants.

DESIGN BY ANDREW FISHER TOMLIN

2 Use a hammock to create a relaxing area shaded by a tree. Secure it to sturdy supports or buy a freestanding cradle.

3 Fire pits provide a dramatic way of heating the garden and can either be sunk into the ground or set on legs like this large, dish-shaped metal unit.

DESIGN BY JOHN WYER

4 Gas-powered outdoor fires offer a clean and convenient way to warm a snug seating area, and the heat output is also easy to control.

DESIGN BY WILSON MCWILLIAM

FUEL OPTIONS

Solid fuel Includes wood, charcoal, peat, coal, fuel tablets, and pellets made from wood. All have different burning characteristics and heat outputs; some are quicker to burn, others lasting longer. Solid fuels are bulky and must be stored in dry conditions to retain combustibility. Use of some solid fuels (eg, coal) is restricted or prohibited in many urban areas due to toxic emissions. Locally sourced wood or charcoal is considered the most eco-friendly option.

Gas Supplied as natural gas or liquefied petroleum gas (LPG) and used for heating, cooking and lighting. Gas is normally supplied as an extension to a domestic system, but must be installed by a qualified engineer and include flues or chimneys to prevent carbon monoxide poisoning. Portable, refillable canisters of propane gas are often used in gardens. Never use gas units in confined spaces.

Electricity Used to provide heat and lighting in gardens, this is the most eco-friendly fuel source. Whether straight from the mains or battery supplies, power is pollution free, clean and instantaneous. Outdoor mains outlets need to be completely weatherproof and installed by a qualified electrician. Check that equipment can be powered from the mains; some heaters require a transformer. And always fit a Residual Current Device (RCD) to shut down units if power leaks or cables are damaged.

Heating systems: options to consider

The following provide heat of different character.

- Open fires: heat is multi-directional, but uncontrolled, and you can choose a range of fuel types, such as wood and charcoal. Fires will need regular cleaning.
- Enclosed fires: generate directional heat, and run on solid fuel or gas, installed by a qualified engineer.
- Chimineas: front-loading open fires of Mexican origin, made from cast iron, aluminium or ceramics.
- Gas patio heaters: controllable propane-fired burners, with a reflector to maximise heat output.
- Electrical radiators: halogen lamps are free standing or attached to parasols, and offer controllable output.

Gas fires like this one in a garden designed by Mandy Buckland must be installed by a qualified engineer

Dining

EATING AL FRESCO is one of life's simple pleasures and with a barbecue or more sophisticated outdoor kitchen equipment, it's easy to cook outside too.

COOKING OUTSIDE

Whatever the size of your plot, be it a tiny courtyard or sprawling country garden, you can include facilities to cook *al fresco*, even perhaps picking your own herbs and harvesting fresh salads and vegetables from beds within easy reach. If you love to cook, consider an outdoor kitchen area, with a gas or electrically-powered oven, hot plate or grill, complete with workspaces, sink and a refrigerator, all sheltered beneath a roofed structure.

If your budget is more limited, a barbecue offers the cheapest and most flexible way to cook outside. You can choose from small charcoal-fired units to larger, more sophisticated wheeled models powered by gas, offering greater control over cooking temperatures. Pizza ovens, which also bake bread, are becoming increasingly popular, or consider units with specialised burners for cooking paella or stir frying Chinese and Thai dishes. Alternatively, you can opt to cook indoors, with the kitchen opening onto a patio for dining. The choice is yours.

> *"When building a kitchen outside, remember to factor in the cost of installing services, such as gas, electricity and water. Restrictions may also apply if your property is listed, or if structures will be close to a boundary."*
>
> JOHN NASH

1 Traditional wood-fired pizza ovens blend easily into a garden setting and can also be used for baking bread and cakes, as well as grilling meats. Although hotter than gas ovens, they take time to reach optimum temperatures.

2 The social hub of your garden, a smart outdoor kitchen needs to be as carefully designed as your indoor facilities, with sufficient space for preparation, storage and seating.

DESIGN BY ANA SANCHEZ-MARTIN

Cooking outside: points to consider

- Decide whether you want to cook indoors and bring food out, or require fixed facilities or flexible wheeled systems that can be moved and stored as required.
- Evaluate how cooking facilities might be best arranged around the seating or dining areas outside and their proximity to the kitchen facilities indoors.
- Consider covering your cooking unit with a fixed, weatherproof canopy to extend its life and allow you to use it throughout the year.
- If you need a fixed power supply, such as gas or electricity, only a qualified technician can legally undertake the installation.
- Carefully research all the options open to you, assessing costs and aftercare, as well as the cooking benefits.
- Ensure outdoor work surfaces are weatherproof.
- Check the guarantee, warranty and after-sales service of the cooking facilities you purchase.
- Consider how cooking equipment and facilities may need to be stored or covered in winter.

3 This elaborate green wall surrounding an outdoor kitchen would be time-consuming to maintain, but illustrates a novel way of growing herbs and salads close to where they're needed.

DESIGN BY PATRICIA FOX

CHOOSING A BARBECUE

Barbecuing is the most popular method of cooking food. Units are usually powered by charcoal or propane gas, and range from small disposable and portable types to fixed, built-in barbecues that form an integral part of the hard landscaping.

Fixed barbecues are usually heated by charcoal, but gas burners are also available, offering more accurate heat control. If catering for up to six people a two-burner gas or medium-sized charcoal unit will suffice, although three- or four-burner models allow you to cook for more. A warming plate or rack and a side burner, available on larger models, are options if you frequently cook for big groups.

Gas grills are powered by propane or natural gas, either using propane gas tanks or natural gas delivered through pipes from the household supply. Some models include infrared rear burners and rotisseries for cooking a wider range of dishes. They are convenient and easy to light and control, while clean-up is minimal – simply turn off the grill and brush the grate.

Charcoal grills are cheaper to buy and run than gas units and come in a range of designs, with hoods and vents to more accurately control the heat. Fired with carbon briquettes or natural lump charcoal, they require little skill to achieve good results. Some models use different fuel types, such as wood.

An African-style hut protects a fully equipped kitchen in a garden designed by John Nash.

KEEPING LIVESTOCK

Small livestock are a practical alternative to traditional household pets and easy to keep in the average garden. They enable children to connect with nature and better appreciate where food comes from but, like all pets, they need constant care to maintain their health. Most also thrive with companions rather than in solitary confinement. Check beforehand for regulations in your household deeds or local authority byelaws that may limit the kind of livestock you can keep. Animals are best penned to keep them under control and chickens need protection from urban foxes. Chickens, which are popular with beginners, need only the space of a guinea pig or rabbit run, especially bantam varieties. Micro-pigs, dwarf goats and sheep require more substantial accommodation and their health care will be more expensive.

Keeping livestock: points to consider

- Ensure you have sufficient space for animals: chickens require 3–4m² per bird; micro pigs/goats need 20m².
- Always buy healthy animals from registered breeders who can also advise on care and welfare.
- Before purchasing, evaluate the cost and time involved in keeping, feeding and caring for animals.
- Consider the cost of veterinary care and identify practices that can deal with your animals.
- Talk to breeders, owners and specialist breed societies about keeping desired livestock.

GROWING YOUR OWN

Many people find growing their own food deeply satisfying and enjoyable. A wide range of crops are easy to grow and will provide you with a regular supply of fresh organic produce. But before you start, consider the time you have to tend your productive patch and the microclimate of your garden, as these factors will impact on your choices.

A productive garden requires a little advance planning. Most vegetables need shelter, good light, fertile soil and moisture. Although warmth is needed to ripen pods, berries and many fruits, salads and some fruit crops, such as gooseberries, currants, black cherries and pears, will grow in shadier sites. Where the soil is infertile or thin, try growing crops in raised beds, which are also useful if you cannot stoop down. If your time is limited, a herb patch, self-fertile apple trees and salads are good choices, and where space is at a premium, grow colourful leafy vegetables, such as lettuces, kale and chard, among your flowers or make an ornamental kitchen garden. This comprises a matrix of beds, often box-edged for structure, containing small fruit trees, vegetables, herbs and flowers.

Growing your own: points to consider

- Ensure you have the requisite conditions for growing fruit, vegetables or herbs.
- Design and cultivate only as much space as you are likely to be able to cope with.
- Grow fruit trees that are partially or fully self-fertile.

1 Chickens are easy to keep and modern coops will suit any style of garden. Besides producing a constant supply of eggs, chickens make amusing pets for adults and children alike.

DESIGN BY DEAKINLOCK

2 Create a potager garden by integrating herbs, fruit and other edible plants into your design.

DESIGN BY AMANDA PATTON

3 Pocket planters provide a versatile way of creating racks of fresh herbs on walls and fences in small gardens.

DESIGN BY MERILEN MENTAAL

- Focus on crops you particularly like that will grow in your conditions.
- Consider growing in raised beds if you have problems stooping.
- Buy a greenhouse to grow tender crops, such as tomatoes, cucumbers and aubergines.
- Choose disease resistant and compact vegetable varieties for small spaces.
- Select fruit trees on dwarfing rootstocks and ready-trained espaliers or cordons to train along walls and fences.
- If serious about growing vegetables, rotate crop types to help prevent the build-up of pests and diseases; specialist publications and websites can provide advice.

3

Playing

DESIGNED FOR FUN, gardens large and small can accommodate a range of play equipment for children and the whole family – just ensure it's safe to use.

OUTDOOR GAMES

Garden games are multi-various and span intellectual pursuits, such as chess, through to traditional games, including football, basketball and badminton. If you have a small garden, consider skittles, boules and quoits, which do not require much space to play. Those with larger gardens could consider a dedicated area of lawn for croquet, bowls or even a putting course.

Vigorous games, such as football and basketball, quickly damage fine lawns so lay a general hard-wearing turf, or a synthetic lawn or hard surface. Dedicated tennis courts will need specialist contractors to install them.

Planting around play zones needs to be robust. Choose shrubs, such as elaeagnus, cherry laurel and cotoneaster, and ground cover, including ivy and vinca, which will regenerate if damaged. Woven willow structures are also ideal for creative play and meld with most garden settings.

Outdoor games: points to consider

- Consider participants' needs and how permanent game or play areas need to be; explore how these areas can be evolved as children grow or your needs change.
- Identify how games or play areas can be integrated into the overall garden design.
- Ensure you have sufficient storage facilities for your sports or play equipment.
- Choose appropriate surfaces for your chosen games.

1

PLAY EQUIPMENT

There is a wide range of products for children's play, but those that offer the greatest scope for adventurous and creative activity, such as swings, slides, climbing frames and trampolines, are most likely to sustain their interest as they grow. Try also to select products that are empathetic to the character of the garden; wooden and handmade equipment is often more durable and visually pleasing than plastic, while existing natural features, such as slopes for slides, can be used to blend play areas into the landscape.

Play equipment: points to consider

- Plan for the future, so play equipment can be substituted as your children's needs change.
- Design areas or zones for sports or games that all the family can enjoy.
- Ensure safety of use with soft or flexible play surfaces and net cages for trampolines.
- Choose natural materials to integrate play equipment into the design.

> *"Play equipment can look unsightly, especially in a small garden. Where possible, screen it with trellis and climbers or, if visibility is important, place low plants around the play area to help soften its appearance."*
> DENISE CADWALLADER

SAFETY FIRST

All play equipment needs to be safe and installed with care. Play surfaces for domestic gardens should comply with safety standard EN1177 and must be self-draining and non-slip. You can use special tiles and other manufactured surfaces, or a thick layer of bark chips (15cm [6in] or more). It is generally recognised that gravel and hard paving are not suitable as surfaces for play areas.

Play equipment in domestic gardens needs to satisfy the British Toy and Hobby Association standard EN718 and also exhibit the CE and Lion mark indicating that it is safe to use. Look for products that are non-toxic and use paint that does not contain lead. Also ensure swings, slides and other equipment are secured firmly to the ground and have no awkward protrusions to cause children harm. Swings should have ropes that do not wear at fixing points and impact-absorbing seats; slides require side guards and guards and hand grips at the top to prevent falls. Climbing frames must be robust and securely fixed to the ground to prevent them toppling. There is currently no British Manufacturing Standard for domestic trampolines, but models with safety pads covering springs, hooks and the frame are best. If purchasing a commercial model it should meet BS EN 13219:2001. Always surround trampolines with a durable safety net, install it on a soft or springy surface, and maintain a safety zone of at least 2.5m (8ft) around the unit.

Utilise natural and artificially created slopes for play equipment such as slides.

1 Outdoor games, such as chess, skittles, boules or quoits, are fun for users of all ages.

DESIGN BY LUCY SOMMERS

2 Swings fit easily into all but the smallest spaces. Make them safe by ensuring they are secured firmly into the ground.

3 Indulge your interests and passions and make them part of the garden experience. Model railways can be artfully integrated into the design to keep reappearing at vantage points; this one is 'parked' at a model station in a shed at night.

DESIGN BY DENISE CADWALLADER

1 When carefully installed, treehouses can become a real asset to the garden, but ensure developments are permitted and neighbours' privacy is not invaded.

DESIGN BY ACRES WILD

2 Children love to make dens, and tents are a delightful way for them to indulge in creative play.

3 Introduce incidental play features for children around the garden, such as this xylophone made from stainless steel.

4 A timber pergola with galvanised metal poles doubles as an exercise frame with rope handles for various routines.

Treehouses: points to consider

- Decide who you want the structure for – children, teenagers or the whole family?
- Locate it to create the best effect, blending it sensitively into the surrounding landscape.
- Purchase from established companies whose products and work is guaranteed.
- Check beforehand for any planning issues and if the tree is listed.
- Agree your design plans with neighbours who are likely to be overlooked.
- Safety is paramount, especially if you plan to create your own structure.

TREEHOUSES

Den making is a compelling proposition for both children and adults! Whether fixed, free standing, elevated on supports or built into a tree, treehouses are exciting features that stand the test of time and become a valuable asset. There are many companies that specialise in creating treehouses, so check online for details of the range of self-assembly kits, ready-made products and bespoke creations on offer. Most structures are crafted from tanalised softwood or durable hardwood, such as oak. They can be painted, but look best when allowed to weather naturally and blend into your garden landscape. Before building a treehouse, ask an arboricultural consultant to check the tree for general health and establish whether it will withstand the weight of the construction.

PLAYHOUSES AND TENTS

Tents and playhouses offer children a special place of their own. Decide whether you want a permanent structure or something temporary, such as a tent, tepee or yurt – children love the novelty of pitching a tent when the weather is fine. Playhouses come in plastic or timber, either as flat-pack kits or ready-made structures, but a more long-lasting and potentially cheaper option is to convert a small garden shed. Tents and other temporary structures add character to the garden but remember if left in place for too long they will kill the grass beneath, so keep moving them to new positions.

Bathing

SWIMMING AND BATHING facilities add shimmering features to a design, and heighten the enjoyment of a garden, providing space for exercise and relaxation.

INSTALLING A SWIMMING POOL

Swimming in your own pool offers unrivalled opportunities for exercise, relaxation, therapy and, most of all, fun. But they can be expensive to install and run, so take time to plan a pool and consider the cost and time of the maintenance required before you buy.

Swimming pools in the UK are generally considered 'permitted development' if not positioned beyond the principle elevation fronting a highway, such as a front garden, but it's worth checking that your proposals meet local regulations just in case. Particularly in temperate areas, pools are best sited in a sunny, sheltered spot, shielded for privacy by hedges or fences.

There are many styles on offer, ranging from formal geometric pools to free-form and naturalistic shapes. Pools can be raised from the ground or partially or completely sunken. Or you can choose an infinity pool (where the water surface seems to flow out seamlessly into the landscape, usually from a dramatic vantage point) or brimming pools. This style will require additional balancing tanks and pumps to maintain the effect.

Pools can be heated to extend usage, especially valuable in cooler areas, but will need covering when not in use and in winter. If the pool is some distance from the house, a changing room may also be needed. This could form an extension to a glazed summerhouse, ideal for relaxing in on cooler days, and for providing shade from hot sun. A garden

building next to a pool also offers the perfect venue for parties and other social occasions.

Prices are influenced by the pool style and specifications, construction materials, which include concrete, fibreglass or vinyl, location, access to the site, and underlying ground conditions. Your supplier will advise you on the costs.

Swimming pools: points to consider

- Balance what you need the pool for with how often it will be used and by whom.
- Shop around for solutions that best meet your needs, and which are appropriate for your site.
- Include all the elements that will make using the pool as comfortable as possible, such as changing facilities, sun terrace and lighting for evening use.
- Consider the additional costs of upkeep and maintaining the pool to high standards of cleanliness.
- Ensure adequate provisions for the safe use of the facility by all age groups and users.
- Employ contractors with expertise in pool construction to build the pool and surrounding landscaping.

"Heat exchange pumps are energy- and cost-effective pool heaters, and consider an electronic dosage system, which accurately monitors and adjusts the chemicals in the water, avoiding unnecessary treatments."
JAMES BASSON OF SCAPE DESIGN

1 A freeform-shaped swimming pool is mirrored by the curves of the lawn, visually anchoring the features together in the space.

DESIGN BY SEAN BUTLER

2 A brimming pool where the water level is continually kept topped up to the edge creates a serene and charismatic feature.

DESIGN BY JAMES BASSON

3 Compact 'endless' exercise pools and swim spas, which allow users to swim against a controllable current, can fit into tiny gardens and courtyards.

4 A changing room, pool and lounge built into a slope allow unimpeded views of the landscape from the house above.

DESIGN BY ACRES WILD

NATURAL SWIMMING POOLS

Natural pools marry the lifestyle attractions of a traditional swimming pool with the environmental attributes of a natural pond, with aquatic plants and wildlife forming an integral part of the system. Rather than using chemical purifiers, water in natural pools is pumped through biological filters and plant roots in an area known as a 'regeneration zone', which keep the water clean, clear and pure enough for bathing. The plants grow in a walled bed, the top of which is 20cm (8in) below the water level. Some natural pools can be heated, depending on the size and technical design, and the surface area available for swimming can be anywhere between 20 to 75 per cent. In small gardens, you could opt for a chlorine-free, unplanted pool, sometimes referred to as a 'living' pool. This uses a system of biological filters, and 100 per cent of the surface area is available for swimming.

A natural pool generally costs as much as a conventional pool to build but, when properly installed in the right location, avoiding trees and shade, the maintenance and running costs are lower. You can also convert a conventional pool into a natural one; existing ponds may also be converted, but you will need to get them evaluated for suitability.

Before committing to a natural pool, investigate manufacturers and suppliers, the range of products on offer, and the various technologies available, as well as guarantees and after-sales service. Also ask to look at mature examples of suppliers' work.

This natural pool, in a garden designed by Wilson McWilliam, provides a chlorine-free swimming experience.

1 An infinity pool conveys a seamless transition between the water and landscape beyond and is best sited where the pool overlooks the sea or a lake, or in an elevated position.

DESIGN BY ANDY STURGEON

2 An automatic pool cover is well worth the extra expense; it helps to keep the water clean and prevents heat from escaping when it is not in use and over winter.

DESIGN BY JANINE PATTISON

3 A sunken hot tub in a timber-decked patio provides breathtaking panoramic views of the seascape beyond. Sinking a pool or tub into a patio integrates it into the setting and enhances the design style.

DESIGN BY TINA VALLIS

4 Hot tubs can be intrusive but the timber cladding on this one melds into the screen behind, transforming it into a decorative design feature. A pergola clad with climbing plants further shrouds the bathing area.

DESIGN BY LOUISE HARRISON-HOLLAND

POOLS FOR SMALL SPACES

Even small gardens can include a pool to add to the enjoyment of the garden. The simplest products are made from moulded plastic or vinyl-lined metal-plated tanks, and models can be sunk into, or partially or fully raised above the ground. For more energetic exercise, consider a lap pool, where swimmers encounter a strong pump-generated current that holds them in position. Other options include spas and plunge pools with heated and jetted water for hydrotherapy or exercise via submerged treadmills. Units can either be dismantled and stored for the winter or remain outdoors as permanent installations, perhaps located in heated garden rooms for year-round use, or under roofed structures to provide shelter in inclement summer weather.

Pools for small spaces: points to consider

- Calculate who is to use the pool, the nature of the activities required and amount of use it will receive.
- If the pool will be temporarily installed for summer use, ensure you have adequate facilities to store it in winter.
- Consider whether it is best sunk into, partially raised or free standing above the ground.
- Determine whether the pool will be on show or shrouded from view with appropriate landscaping and plants, which will need to be planned into the build.
- Assess the maintenance and running costs of the pool.
- Purchase products from a reputable company that offers guarantees and after-sales service.

CHOOSING A HOT TUB

Hot tubs are popular and suitable for most gardens, especially when used to complement other bathing facilities or where a swimming pool would be too large or expensive. The tanks of temperature-controlled water include submerged seating and adjustable jets that create a range of sensations. Units made from moulded plastic or wood are widely available, and they can be freestanding or submerged into the ground, often inset into raised timber-decked patios or dedicated bathing areas. LED lighting facilitates their use at night. Hot tub prices are determined by the design, functions, and degree of innovation, but also remember to factor in the on-going costs of chemicals and maintenance.

Hot tubs: points to consider

- Appraise the size and design of various units for one that best suits your purpose and style of garden.
- Decide where it would be best located to work in concert with other features and your garden setting.
- Determine whether it should be free standing or sunk into decking or a patio.
- Evaluate the time involved and cost of running and maintaining the unit to requisite standards of health and safety – a hot tub can be a health hazard if the unit and water are not clean.
- Consider a roofed or covered structure to extend its use.
- Always buy from reputable companies that provide a guarantee or warranty and after-sales service.

GARDENS WITH
A CONSCIENCE

Sustainable solutions

MINIMISING NEGATIVE EFFECTS on the environment when creating a garden is easy if you recycle and reuse materials, or use those that are sourced ethically.

LOWERING CARBON FOOTPRINTS

We are all aware that the planet's natural resources are under intolerable pressure from over-exploitation, and while some aspects of garden-making tread lightly on the earth from an energy and carbon usage perspective, creating an outdoor space can contribute to the problem. Extracting desirable rocks and minerals for decoration, hardwood timber for furniture, peat for horticultural practices and fossil fuels for heating all make significant demands on resources. Imported products also expend energy when transported long distances to consumers.

Well-designed gardens can be created utilising products from low-carbon technologies and manufacturing processes, but it is incumbent on all of us to play our part by reducing fossil fuel usage and recycling and repurposing materials where we can. Many designers can advise you on ways to produce a beautiful outdoor room without impacting on the local or wider environment, or, if designing the space yourself, follow the tips overleaf to minimise your carbon footprint.

"Using reclaimed landscaping materials is a really simple and effective way to bring a depth of character and soul to a space. They are also perfect for creating a period look, and are great for the environment."

CHRIS GUTTERIDGE

ETHICALLY SOURCING MATERIALS

While some landscape materials are home-produced, others are sourced from abroad because they have desirable qualities or can be extracted more cheaply, or both. Although the popularity of high quality, low-cost stone paving, particularly sandstone, slate and marble from India and the Far East, is understandable, the price often reflects the exploitative practices of mining companies. UNESCO and other charities have highlighted these industries' disregard for workers' safety, deplorable rates of pay, and use of underage workers, including young children. To ensure importers have agreed to a code of fair practice for quarry workers, check that your suppliers are part of the Ethical Trade Initiative (ETI).

Unsolicited importation of tropical hardwoods is also of concern, with tropical rainforests plundered to satiate the global market. Initiatives such as the Forestry Stewardship Council (FSC) scheme have established chains of accountability that ensure only trees ethically sourced from managed plantations are used. So, before purchasing, check that products are part of this scheme and suppliers are able to provide documentary evidence to support their claims.

Recycled stone paving lends a timeless appearance.

1 Use of local materials can invest a design with parochial charm and may also be a requirement in a listed property or conservation area.

DESIGN BY IAN KITSON

2 A linear pattern of stone slabs inset into gravel creates a striking effect and can be created easily with secondhand materials.

DESIGN BY CHRIS GUTTERIDGE

3 Ensure hardwood furniture is made from sustainably sourced timber, best identified through a recognised accreditation scheme, such as the Forestry Stewardship Council (FSC) initiative.

DESIGN BY ANDREW FISHER TOMLIN

4 Recycled and repurposed materials, such as pine cones, can be used as a mulch to control weeds and conserve moisture, while stone chips make a decorative and functional path.

Tips to protect the environment

- Use power tools and machinery that work efficiently and use solar-powered or wind-powered equipment where you can.
- Select ethically-sourced products using internationally recognised schemes that provide a chain of custody from source to consumer (*see p.141*)
- Recycle or re-purpose secondhand items or use products made from recycled materials to help personalise your design or create a sense of place.
- Compost organic household and garden waste to help improve soil rather than buying commercial products.
- Harvest and store rainwater in water butts to irrigate plants and replenish pools, or create rain gardens to help prevent flash flooding (*see p.147*).

RECYCLING AND REPURPOSING

The culture of recycling and reusing objects and materials to create something new and exciting is deeply engrained in the way gardeners and many designers work. While much is prosaically practical, such as pruned stems used to support plants, opportunities abound for repurposing or upcycling items to make decorative features, so consider whether it is worth buying a new and expensive feature, when you may be able to craft a similar item at a fraction of the cost. And if creating a period garden, incorporate salvaged materials, which are perfect for a time-worn look. Also remember that

recycled products are not just suitable for rustic, informal or country garden designs; chic contemporary furniture and accessories made from recycled metals and plastics are now widely available for modern gardens too.

The range of products made from reconstituted materials includes paving, tables and chairs, decking and architectural features. If your local DIY store doesn't stock them, take a look on the internet. Local architectural salvage yards are a good place to start your search for old bricks, paving slabs, timber, ornamental glass and outdoor lighting, as well as decorative ornaments, sculpture and containers from all periods, from Victorian to modern day. You may also discover quirky items to add an individual touch to your design, or objects you can breathe new life into. Sales and auctions are also good sources of decorative pieces. Some specialise in expensive antiques, while others offer a more eclectic range of products at more affordable prices.

As well as bought items, you can also reuse household products. Old pots and pans make ornamental containers, and furniture can also be given new life when treated with coloured preservatives or painted to create a period feel or Bohemian character. Domestic skips and community recycling centres are often useful hunting grounds for secondhand objects and materials; out of courtesy, always ask permission before taking anything from a skip. Depending on your design style, industrial materials can make interesting and quirky features. Sections of concrete pipe, cable drums, metal sheeting and plastic or metal barrels can all be pressed into use. Manufacturers are often happy to give away waste products or ends of line, but always check what they were used for to ensure they are suitable for your intended purpose.

USING LOCAL RESOURCES

Choosing local materials is one of the most efficient ways to lower your carbon footprint. Always make the best of what the site offers, conserving and reusing as much endemic material as you can. Moving topsoil and rubble is expensive, so reuse it on site if possible, unless it is badly degraded or contaminated. Rubble can always be crushed to create

soakaways, or used as footings or sub-bases. Try to improve the soil in your garden, rather than importing new, and use local materials, such as stone and brick, to generate sense of place and anchor your scheme into the landscape. You will probably find sources of similar secondhand materials close to home too.

When possible, use local services and facilities to help create your design, making the most of local craftsman to create features for your garden, as they are more likely to have skills in using the materials you have chosen. And take time to visit local art galleries or arts communities to source people who can fashion unique decorative items to add character and individuality.

1 Recycled timber, ideal as a foil for plants, has a rustic and weather-worn look. Use tar-free sleepers for steps and raised beds, or informal seating.

DESIGN BY ACRES WILD

2 Galvanised metal water tanks make eye-catching features in modern and rustic settings.

DESIGN BY DEAKIN LOCK

3 Almost anything that holds compost can be used to grow plants; just ensure they have drainage holes and select plants that will suit the chosen articles.

4 When stacked on top of one another, recycled metal canisters make an exciting living wall of herbs and vegetables.

5 Offcuts from the timber industry and corten steel have been used for dramatic effect to create these chequerboard walls in a small courtyard. The walls link with the other geometric forms in the design.

DESIGN BY PAUL HENSEY

Green technologies

PLANTED ROOFS AND WALLS help to insulate buildings and attract wildlife, while choosing solar-powered items reduces our dependence on fossil fuels.

GREENING A ROOF

Although an ancient technique, covering roofs with plants is enjoying a resurgence of interest, fuelled by the need to increase or conserve biodiversity, slow rainwater runoff, insulate buildings, and create a social space, as well as providing visual interest. Before you start, consider what you want to achieve from your roof garden, as this will determine the approach and cost. While greening the roof of a small shed can be a simple DIY project, larger schemes will need the services of a specialist contractor. Planning permission may be required, especially on period or listed properties, and a qualified engineer will also need to assess the load-bearing capacity of the building.

To flourish, green roof plants must have sunlight, moisture, drainage, nutrients and aeration, and if any factors are lacking or the species chosen are inappropriate for the conditions, the scheme is likely to fail. Green roofs vary from 'lightweight extensive', usually involving pre-grown mats of drought-tolerant, hardy succulents, such as sedum, through to 'intensive', with more than 200mm (8in) of substrate and bespoke planting designed to meet the site conditions. Most extensive and many intensive green roofs are supplied as complete systems from specialists.

1 Ideal for garden rooms, pavilions and sheds, planted roofs help to help control the flow of water into drains and increase wildlife habitats for insects and birds.

"The best plants for sunny roofs are sedums, which are drought- and wind-tolerent – just don't over water them. Low-growing alliums also work well. For shady sites, try Polypodium vulgare *and* Sedum ellacombianum.*"*
PAUL HENSEY

CHOOSING GREEN WALL SYSTEMS

Methods of covering vertical structures with plants involve two basic approaches, namely green façades and living walls. Green façades involve climbing plants growing on a vertical structure. Their stems may require supports, such as stainless steel or wooden trellis, meshwork, or cabling, or you can opt for self-supporting climbers, such as Boston ivy and climbing hydrangea. Green façades can be used to provide privacy or security, or to screen or embellish parking lots, patios, walkways or sitting areas. Plants are generally rooted in beds at the base of the structure, or in self-contained planters, also known as 'living curtains' or 'green screens'. Depending on climate, choice of species and growing conditions, green façades may take several seasons to achieve maturity.

Living wall systems or 'vertical gardens', as they are sometimes known, are composed of panels, modules, or bags, usually attached to a wall or free-standing framework (*see page 65*), which hold non-climbing plants, rather like a series of windowboxes. Modules are variously made of plastic, polystyrene, synthetic fabric, or clay, and can support a great diversity of plants. Flowers, herbs, vegetables and fruit often feature in living walls, planted in a range of compost types, including coir, crushed bark, expanded clay granules, gravel, and perlite, often in blended mixes. Watering and feeding systems are essential for the plants' long-term survival, with computer controlled units providing the best solution for large installations.

This simple modular system by Vertigarden offers the home gardener an easy option for a small green wall.

SOLAR POWER IN THE GARDEN

An option for lights, pumps and other small accessories, solar-powered features are inexpensive, easy to install and increasingly sophisticated in design and style. Units are either driven directly from a solar panel or via rechargeable batteries, and to work efficiently, they need constant direct light. If units are set in shadier sites, the running times will be short or the power source too low.

Lighting units vary from small, glowing pathway markers to patio and security lights that use LED bulbs, although these lights are not as powerful as fluorescent or halogen types. Solar power is also used for water features and fountains, either driving the pump directly, meaning it cannot run at night, or via a battery for greater flexibility. Water flow is not as powerful as that from a mains-driven pump, but usually sufficient for ripple effects or low jets.

2 Solar panels can be used to power garden equipment and facilities, such as lighting and water features. Improvements in technology will continue to increase their effectiveness.

3 Solar-powered lighting can be installed in every type of garden and located wherever needed, as long as the units that absorb energy are positioned in a sunny area.

Managing water

KEY TO PLANTS' WELLBEING, water is critical to any planted scheme, so take action to ensure this precious resource does not simply go down the drain.

WATER WISDOM

Of all precious resources that can be harvested, rain water is probably the most squandered. While rainfall replenishes soil moisture and provides humidity to keep plants hydrated, in towns and cities most simply goes down the drain. In addition, urbanisation has greatly increased the area covered by impermeable surfaces, so that intense rainfall quickly overloads drains and sewers, causing flash flooding. With rainfall patterns predicted to become more intense and urban living expanding rapidly, the situation is set to become worse unless these issues are addressed. We can all help to reduce the problem by limiting the amount of impervious hard surfacing in our gardens, particularly in front gardens used for parking cars. Permeable materials, such as gravel and unjointed paving, will help storm water percolate away, while planted beds also soak up excesses. In addition, rainwater collected in butts or underground tanks not only supplies irrigation for plants and replenishes ponds and water features, it can also fill toilet systems and run other domestic systems in the house. Water collection can be simple or sophisticated, and may include pumps, purification equipment and drip-irrigation systems.

2 A small rain garden in a domestic plot collects water from a summerhouse roof and overflows into a soakaway in front of the patio.

3 Water butts offer a good way of storing rainwater from garden buildings. Larger volumes can be stored in underground tanks and used when the butts run dry.

4 Gravel surfaces allow rain to percolate slowly into the ground, rather than run into the drains. A purpose-made mesh grid holds the gravel in place, even in areas of high traffic such as driveways.

5 Heavy gauge metal tracks provide vehicular access to a front garden, while groundcover planting and gravel collect rainwater and allow it to soak away naturally into the ground.

1 Rainwater from buildings and structures is stored in interconnected tanks in this rain garden, helping to prevent flash flooding and providing a habitat for aquatic plants and wildlife.

RAIN GARDENS

Gardens or parts of the garden that act as a sump or reservoir for the temporary storage of storm water are known as 'rain gardens'. They are already familiar features in areas of the world that experience regular storm events, as they enable excess water to slowly discharge, evening out the flow into drains and sewers and preventing flash flooding. With the increasing uncertainty of weather patterns, these gardens are now being included in more temperate parts of the world too. As well as alleviating flooding, rain gardens bring additional benefits, supporting wildlife by providing refuges for amphibians such as frogs and newts, as well as drinking and bathing water for small animals and birds. They can be beautiful features, too, supporting a host of ornamental marshland and bog plants.

To create a rain garden, you will need to consider a number of factors, including where the rain will be diverted from, such as the roof of a shed, summerhouse or garage, and where best to site the sump area. If attempting a large scheme, where water is taken from the house roof for example, check the capacity and siting of the sump required with a qualified engineer or ask an experienced practitioner for advice before you begin.

Supporting wildlife

NATURAL HABITATS are under pressure and many are rapidly diminishing, but gardens can help alleviate this problem, providing refuges, food and water for wildlife.

CREATING HABITATS

Gardens have been identified by scientists as important sanctuaries for wildlife, with both country, town and city plots contributing habitats that intensive agricultural practices and urbanisation have erased. Research suggests that no particular garden style is better than another, with those comprising a strong, geometric, but well-planted layout able to cradle just as much wildlife as naturalistic or freeform schemes. What is important is the diversity and density of the gardens in any given area. Collectively, they create a host of opportunities for sheltering and feeding birds, animals and insects, as well as providing the right conditions for breeding. You can make your garden more wildlife friendly with plants that help sustain and support birds, insects and small animals. Recent research has also shown that many exotic species are equally or even more beneficial to wildlife than indigenous flora, particularly at the beginning and end of the year when native food plants are scarce. So, simply create a range of habitats, provide water and the right plants, and wildlife will follow.

1 Whether formal or informal in design, a pond will always attract wildlife. Where possible, include a slope or beach area on at least one side of your water feature to allow small animals and birds easy access.

DESIGN BY CHERYL CUMMINGS

2 Provide a succession of nectar- and pollen-rich flowering plants for bees and other pollinators throughout the year; seeds for birds in the autumn; and dead stems for beneficial overwintering insects.

DESIGN BY TRACY FOSTER

3 Water bodies of varying depths, interspersed by beach areas and lush planting, are colonised by all sorts of wildlife, creating a major habitat in this urban garden, as well as a beautiful feature to admire.

DESIGN BY FIONA STEPHENSON

4 Even temporary sources of fresh water, such as dips and hollows, will attract amphibians in spring, but also try to create other damp spots for them to hide in at other times of the year, such as dense planting or log piles.

BOOSTING BEE POPULATIONS

Bees are among the most important plant pollinators, and without their activities most of our fruit and vegetable crops would not exist. This is why the recent decline in honey bee populations, known as colony collapse disorder, is causing international concern and the reasons for it are being urgently researched. All garden owners can help to support bee populations by providing food and habitats for a whole range of species, of which there are around 250 in the UK alone, made up of 225 species of solitary bee, 24 types of bumblebee and one form of honeybee.

Some bee species are gregarious, living in colonies, while others are solitary, living alone or in small groups. The various types also have different habitat needs. Ground-dwelling bees inhabit abandoned rodent holes, areas under sheds and compost heaps, while other species nest in grass, trees, bird boxes, or crevices in brick walls, so by including some of these features you can increase the variety and number of bees that take up residence in your garden.

Plants that attract bees are rich in pollen and nectar, with different flowers attracting different kinds of bee. However, those with single flowers are best, as plants with double flowers have no pollen- and nectar-carrying parts. Bee-friendly plants often exhibit labels with a bee logo to help you identify them at the garden centre. You can also keep bees yourself by joining the British Bee Keeper's Association, or support the charity Bumblebee Conservation Trust, which undertakes research and conservation.

Opened-flowered dahlias are magnets for bees

Tips to make your garden wildlife-friendly

- A small pond or water feature will dramatically increase the range and abundance of visiting wildlife, especially amphibians, insects and birds. Try to use rainwater to fill ponds and include a shallow beach to allow creatures easy access in and out of the water.
- Shrubs, trees and evergreen climbers provide shelter and places for birds to roost and nest. Also include nest boxes of various sizes to attract a range of bird species.
- Create areas of longer grass to provide nesting sites for butterflies, bees and other insects.
- Make piles of logs and branches to act as refuges for beetles and other wood-dwelling insects.
- Don't be too quick to repoint brickwork in old walls as these make ideal overwintering sites for solitary bees.
- Leave herbaceous plants intact in the autumn and winter, rather than cutting them down. Seedheads provide sources of food for birds and hollow stems offer overwintering sites for insects, such as ladybirds.
- Try to use organic or wildlife-friendly methods and products to tackle pests and diseases, or spot-treat problems as they occur.

1 Fresh water attracts birds to drink and bathe, but remember to clean out dishes regularly. Birds also need a range of seasonal foods, such as grubs in spring to feed their young and fat-based food in autumn and winter.

2 Insects, such as solitary bees, live and overwinter in holes in the ground or in plant stems. So-called 'bee-hotels' can be bought ready-made or created with bundles of plant stems tied together and hung up in full sun.

SUPPLYING FOOD AND WATER

The key to sustaining a wide range of wildlife in your garden is to provide a variety of food. This will help to establish a natural food chain, with insects and invertebrates that feed on plants and other tiny animals also attracting larger omnivores, such as birds, frogs and hedgehogs, that feed on them.

Birds need different foods to suit their changing needs through the year. Insects are critical for raising young chicks, while berries and seeds are important in autumn and winter to add to birds' fat reserves, sustaining them through the colder months. Holly and cotoneaster attract thrushes and blackbirds, red wings and field fares can be lured with hawthorn, and teasel seeds are loved by goldfinches and buntings. Supplementary foods can include dried mealworms in spring, seeds and fruits in summer and suet and fat balls in winter.

Other types of wildlife have different food requirements at various stages of their life-cycles. Butterfly and moth larvae eat different plant-parts to the winged adults, which feed on nectar from flowers while their young consume the leaves of native plant species. As bees and pollinating insects, such as hover and drone flies, take nectar and pollen from a variety of plants, provide a succession of flowers throughout the year, especially in late winter and late autumn, when blooms are in short supply.

Ponds and pools attract a wide range of wildlife, which uses them for drinking, bathing and breeding. You can also provide fresh water in shallow containers, ensuring they are cleaned out every few days to prevent disease.

3 While trees, shrubs and hedges provide sites for birds to roost and nest, bird boxes will still prove attractive to many; the size of the holes at the front influences the species of bird that will use them.

4 Walls created from rustic logs not only provide a textural screen to subdivide your space, but also offer homes for wildlife, including amphibians, bees, beetles and burrowing insects.

Shared spaces

FROM COMMUNITY GARDENS to those in schools and hospitals, shared outdoor spaces bring people together to enjoy and benefit from the plants and wildlife.

COMMUNAL AND COMMUNITY GARDENS

With high-value inner city land always under pressure for development, individual gardens are not always possible or feasible. Communal gardens are often a solution, offering unified spaces available for all residents to enjoy. Landscaped areas around housing developments are likely to be privately owned and maintained by a contractor to an agreed standard, and the use of space can be passive, such as sitting and communing with neighbours, friends or family, or interactive, where designated areas are identified for residents to cultivate their own plants.

Communal gardens provide a wonderful opportunity for people to interact with nature and develop new skills, while promoting neighbourliness and a sense of community. They may also be a catalyst for social groups that share resources, skills and interests. If you want to develop a garden, whether on a patio outside a block of flats or area of ground around your home, check first that there are no restrictions from your landlord or housing trust on the use of the land and what you can grow. Ask your local authority and look at the deeds of your property to find out what is permissible.

Community gardens are slightly different from communal gardens. Most are run by not-for-profit groups or charities, with local communities frequently adopting spaces that have been physically degraded or neglected, or parks and amenity areas that can no longer be financially supported by local authorities. Movements such as

Transition Towns and Sustain also run community gardens and orchards to make a cultural difference, encouraging people to grow and sell their own vegetables close to home.

Community gardens can also play an important role in fulfilling a social need, providing a club for those who are physically, mentally or socially disadvantaged, where individuals can gain confidence and develop new skills through horticulture and garden-making.

> *"Community gardens are not about the final design but about the process of gardening. However, it's best to start with a basic framework of paths, hedges and trees to divide up the space for a range of activities."*
>
> JOHN WYER

1 A well designed and maintained communal thoroughfare not only offers an attractive amenity, but also increases respect for the space.

2 Previously a foreboding haunt used by drug dealers, this alley is now a beautiful space managed by the local community.

3 A striking design, with geometric paths, seats and green spaces, sets the tone for this office and apartment complex.

4 Many communal gardens are tended by friends' groups and community associations, enabling ownership the space.

ALLOTMENTS

Most towns and cities, and even country areas, include land set aside by the local authority for allotments, enabling local people with small gardens or those living in flats to cultivate a wide range of crops and ornamental plants. Allotment sites and the groups that run them vary enormously, with some overseen directly by local authorities, others by local societies that act as agents for the council or are self governing. These societies often provide additional facilities, such as a social centre or bulk-buying of horticultural products and sundries for site users.

The popularity of growing produce has led to a shortage of allotments in some areas, so you may need to add your name to a waiting list. But before taking one on, consider the time you have available to cultivate it. While producing your own fresh food has its appeal, an allotment is also hard work to maintain, so ask if you can develop just part of a plot or share one with friends if your time is limited.

5 While allotments offer opportunities to grow fresh food, they require commitment and time to maintain them.

6 Many allotment sites are in multicultural neighbourhoods, promoting the exchange of crops and skills from different cultures.

SCHOOL DEVELOPMENTS

With horticulture now part of the national curriculum, schools are establishing gardens as a stage for practical study. The catalyst has been the widespread realisation that many school children do not know where food comes from, combined with a decline in the knowledge and skills needed to grow and cultivate plants. Gardening can be used across a wide range of other studies, too, including mathematics, biology, geography, physics and chemistry, as well as tuning children into seasonal rhythms, and increasing exercise, teamwork and personal development.

If your school does not have a garden and you want to create one, you can make representation through school governors or the senior management team. Important issues to consider when setting up such a garden include site access, and the allocation of responsibilities for the on-going maintenance during term times and holiday periods,

particularly in summer. When selecting plants, opt for those that grow and yield quickly during term times, such as salads, or carry on through summer and are harvested in autumn, including pumpkins and squashes. Apples and pears that ripen in September and October are also useful. Tall sunflowers, willow or hazel for weaving and memorable aromatic plants, such as sage, rosemary and lavender, are also fun to grow. And try to follow organic growing techniques to avoid the use of chemical pesticides.

HOSPICE GARDENS

Designers are increasingly being asked to provide creative solutions for hospice gardens, either through charitable organisations or directly through hospice management teams. The value of gardens for those with terminal conditions cannot be underestimated. They provide opportunities to connect with nature and allow patients

1 Gardens in schools should be stimulating and interactive environments, and also encourage children to explore and understand the natural world and our place within it.

DESIGN BY JOANNA HERALD

2 A wild flower meadow has been installed in the grounds of this hospice, allowing users to enjoy the wildlife and flowers. Meadows are also relatively easy to maintain once established.

DESIGN BY CHRIS PARSONS

3 Tactile, aromatic and visually stimulating plants decorate this tranquil space for residents and families of a Maggie's Cancer Care centre in London.

DESIGN BY DAN PEARSON

4 Rich and visually stimulating planting are the hallmarks of the design at this orthopaedic centre, offering residents and staff a space to relax.

DESIGN BY JULIA FOGG

to enjoy the fresh air and sunlight, as well as providing beautiful spaces to meet with loved ones.

Designs need to accommodate wheel chair or disabled access, provide shelter from the elements and be accessible to a number of patients at any one time, with plenty of seating. Raised beds, perhaps with integral seating are often included, enabling plants to be viewed up close and cultivated with minimum effort. Designers also include sensory plants, allowing direct interaction with them, using touch, smell and sight to evoke memories and a sense of well-being. Hospice gardens must also provide visual interest all year round, and look good when viewed from above, encouraging residents and others to visit.

Many hospice gardens are self-funded or supported by charitable trusts, such as the Lottery, but budgets are very tight. So if you love gardening and have the time and skills, contact your local hospice and offer your services.

GARDEN DESIGNS FOR HOSPITALS

Well-designed landscapes and gardens staged in hospital grounds make a valuable contribution to the perceived and actual quality of the facilities, as well as augmenting the range of ancillary services they provide. Research also shows that being outside in a green natural environment has benefits for both physical and mental health, prompting more hospitals to install gardens. Some hospitals have commissioned stand-alone gardens for patients and their visitors to enjoy, while others have integrated planted spaces into the overall landscaping of the site, often in areas close to main thoroughfares, the entranceway and car parks.

The design of a hospital garden needs to be bold and provide visual interest all year round; it must also look good when viewed from surrounding windows, which is how many patients and staff will experience it. Simple yet imposing planting designs tend to work best, and schemes should be easily maintained, as funding is often limited; designers often use land sculpting or the creative use of turf, which offers maximum visual interest at minimal cost.

Some hospitals also use their gardens for creative and therapeutic activities for patients. For example, cancer patients and those suffering from spinal and other physical injuries, can be helped through a range of gardening practices. Although directed by professionals, many institutions depend on volunteers to support these activities, with training for such schemes provided by the hospital staff.

A garden for sufferers of spinal injuries by Cleve West

REALISING
YOUR DESIGN

You can create your own garden design, or call in a professional designer, who will undertake a site survey, present solutions for your plot, and produce a detailed plan such as this one.

DESIGN BY SUE ADCOCK

Assessing your plot

BEFORE YOU START designing, take time to evaluate your site carefully to ensure your proposals will suit your garden's aspect and soil conditions.

First things first

If you are designing the garden yourself, first identify what you want to achieve and note down the features you want to keep and those you would like to change or remove. The most uplifting thing to keep in mind is that all plots have potential and some of the most beautiful gardens have been produced from the most challenging sites.

Important factors to take into account include the garden's aspect and soil type, which will determine the best sites for sitting areas and the plants suited to your conditions. Assessing these factors is not difficult, but if you need advice, a professional designer can conduct a full site survey.

Aspect and climate

The geographical location of your garden will steer the options open to you. Record the way the sun tracks across the sky during the day, and how the prevailing wind and rain impacts on the site. While you cannot change the garden's aspect and the climatic conditions, you can mitigate their effects. A hot and sunny south-facing garden, for example, can be enhanced with shaded areas and drought-tolerant plants, while features that increase light levels, such as reflective walls or water, offer good solutions for north-facing plots. Also consider the influence of buildings, structures and trees, and note how much shade they cast and shelter they provide, and try to use these features to benefit your design.

Soil quality

Your soil type has a significant bearing on the plants that will thrive in your garden, since it supplies moisture, nutrients, space to develop and anchorage for the roots.

The chemical balance of the soil affects the availability of nutrients and the plants you can grow. It can be assessed using a soil testing kit, which determines the soil's pH value, a scale that measures acidity. Neutral soils have a pH of 7, acid soils measure pH6 or below and alkaline soils have a value up to pH8 or above. Acid-loving plants include rhododendrons, azaleas and camellias, while clematis, hebes and lavender like alkaline soils, others are not too fussed, but check plant labels for specific requirements. Soil testing kits usually indicate pH with a simple colour chart, and test the soil across your site as it may vary from area to area.

Soil structure is another important factor to check. Heavy clay soils are dense, difficult to work, and prone to waterlogging in winter and baking hard in summer. However, they are also moisture-retentive and have a high nutrient content. Sandy soils are gritty and free draining; they lose water and nutrients very quickly and many are acidic in nature. Thin, highly alkaline chalky soils are also prone to drying out; gardens on chalk are best designed with plants adapted to the conditions.

Soils in urban and new build gardens are often compacted and degraded with building rubble. These and heavy clay soils can be improved by breaking up the compaction with a fork or rotavator, and adding organic matter, such as well-rotted compost or manure. This will improve the soil structure, reducing waterlogging and allowing you to grow a wider range of plants. If your soil is badly degraded, raised beds filled with good quality top soil from a reputable supplier may be the

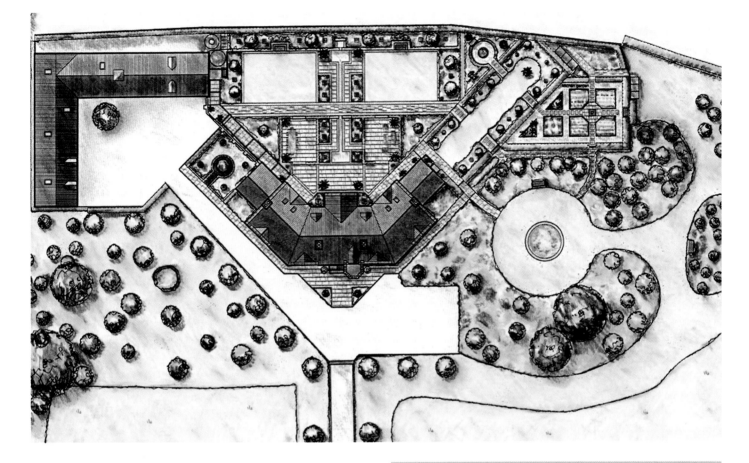

answer. Sandy soils can also be improved with organic matter, which helps increase their capacity to hold water and nutrients. Although all soils can be improved, for long-term success, select plants that suit their basic characteristics.

Create a scale plan

If you are designing your own plot, rather than employing an expert, you may find a scale plan useful. Use a scale that enables you to work up a design on an A2 or A1 sheet, depending on the size of your plot. You can obtain a scale rule and paper at professional art shops. Alternatively, if you are proficient on computers, try a garden design software package. You may also be able to lift the general shape of your plot from an OS map, from shots taken from upstairs windows or even from Google Earth. Alternatively, create a simple plan by measuring your site and noting its dimensions. For more complex sites on different levels, or with unusual features, call in a professional designer to conduct a full site survey and draw up a detailed scale plan.

LOCAL PLANNING AND BUILDING REGULATIONS

To prevent infringement of local planning and environmental laws, you may need to seek planning permission for a new development, particularly if your redesign involves major changes to the landscape or your property is listed. Check the deeds to the house for any clauses governing changes in use or structural alterations. Changing access to the site from a main road will also need planning permission and may incur the costs of local authority contractors to undertake the work. Excavations and significant alterations to the ground level may also require council approval, or the services of a civil engineer. Trees may be subject to preservation orders – approval for work on them will be needed in advance and significant financial penalties incurred if it is not. Permissions may take time to obtain, so factor them into the schedule; designers can advise you and may help seek approvals on your behalf.

Commissioning a designer

CREATING A GARDEN of real quality requires vision, sensitivity, skill and experience, so take time to choose the designer that best suits your expectations and needs.

Making your choice

When selecting a designer, first take a look at their portfolio, and then, if their approach is in accord with your ideas, arrange an initial meeting. Remember, too, that some designers only take commissions local to their area, while others work nationally or even internationally.

Discuss with your designer the area of the garden to be designed and the extent of the commission, agreeing which of the following services will be included:

- Complete garden design.
- Planting design, including detailed planting plans.
- Additional drawings for walls, paving or decking designs.
- Specialist elements, such as water features, green walls, roof gardens, sculpture or lighting.
- Obtaining tenders, nominating contractors and monitoring projects to completion.
- Cost estimates for agreed works and plants.
- The supply of plants.
- Construction work and supply of building materials.
- Ongoing maintenance of the garden after installation.

Agreeing the fee

Talk through ideas, requirements and budget constraints with your designer to determine a programme of work and a clear understanding of the total cost of the consultancy service, including expenses, fees for contractors, and the cost of materials and plants. Agreement between you

A designer will help unlock the potential of your site in ways you may not have considered. Evaluate work from a number of different designers first before choosing someone with the flair and skill that suits your needs.

This dramatic curved water garden, set off by lush planting and meadows, shows how a professional garden designer can take a prosaic landscape, such as derelict tennis courts (top right), and transform it into a breathtaking, inspirational space.

DESIGN BY IAN KITSON

and your designer can take the form of an exchange of letters or the JCLI Consultancy Agreement, which is a specialised contract supplied by the Society of Garden Designers (SGD), designed to make sure both parties fully understand the scope of the project. Charges for services vary from designer to designer and accurate estimates are only possible once you have agreed what is required. Fees tend to be between 10 and 20 per cent of the total cost of the garden. Planting plans and finding contractors and monitoring work to completion may be charged separately, so agree this with your designer at the outset.

Fees can be charged in different ways, and may be a lump sum or percentage of the total cost of the garden build, or a daily rate. In addition to the fee for design, you may have to reimburse expenses such as travel and telephone costs, and payments made to third parties by the designer, which could include planning application fees, land surveys and soil testing.

The Society of Garden Designers

Registered members of the Society of Garden Designers are approved professional garden designers. They have passed the Society's adjudication interview, and their skills have been assessed. Many have additionally passed professional garden design courses and all have a minimum of two years' practical experience. Only registered members can use MSGD (Member of Society of Garden Designers) or FSGD (Fellow) after their name. Registered members work under the Code of Conduct and Constitution of the Society. They are listed on the website, www.sgd.org.uk, where you can search for a designer by name, postcode, county or country.

Directory of designers

Further details for all registered Society of Garden Designers members listed here can be found on the SGD website, **www.sgd.org.uk**, together with their addresses, telephone numbers, and the locations in which they work.
If no website is listed, please refer to the SDG website for contact details.

Key to Abbreviations
MSGD: Fully Registered Member of the Society of Garden Designers
FSGD: Fellow of the Society of Garden Designers

1. **Sue Adcock MSGD**
   www.sueadcockdesigns.com

2. **Marie-Louise Agius MSGD**
   www.balston.co.uk

3. **Rosemary Alexander FSGD**
   www.rosemaryalexander.co.uk

4. **Ross Allan MSGD**
   www.rossallandesigns.com

5. **Irma Ansell MSGD**
   www.bucksgardendesign.co.uk

6. **Susan Ashton MSGD**
   www.susanashton.co.uk

7. **Dana Assinder MSGD**
   www.dkagardendesign.co.uk

8. **Paul Baines MSGD**
   www.paul-baines.co.uk

9. **Michael Ballam MSGD**
   www.edinburghgardendesign.net

10. **Sophie Barclay MSGD**
    Contact the SGD for details

11. **James Basson MSGD**
    www.scapedesign.com

12. **Louisa Bell MSGD**
    www.thelovelygarden.co.uk

13. **Mathew Bell MSGD**
    www.mygardens.co.uk

14. **Anna Benn MSGD**
    Visit the SGD website for contact details

15. **Lee Bestall MSGD**
    www.InspiredGardenDesign.co.uk

16. **Sarah Bicknell MSGD**
    www.sauterelle.co.uk

17. **Helen Billetop FSGD**
    www.cgd-landscape-design.com

18. **Jill Billington FSGD**
    Visit the SGD website for contact details

19. **Beverley Blackburn MSGD**
    www.beverleyblackburn.com

20. **Alison Blakey MSGD**
    www.alison-gardendesigner.com

21. **Sol Blytt-Jordens MSGD**
    Visit the SGD website for contact details

22. **Miriam Book MSGD**
    www.gardenbook.co.uk

23. **Lenore Boothby MSGD**
    www.bartongrangelandscapes.co.uk

24. **Dan Bowyer MSGD**
    www.fishertomlin.com

25. **Jane Brockbank MSGD**
    www.janebrockbank.com

26. **John Brookes MBE FSGD**
    www.john-brookes-garden-design.com

27. **Angela Brooke-Smith MSGD**
    www.flowerfusions.co.uk

28. **Gilly Brown MSGD**
    www.gillybrown.com

29. **Mandy Buckland MSGD**
    www.greencubelandscapes.co.uk

30. Sean Butler MSGD
www.cube1994.com

31. Denise Cadwallader FSGD
www.garden-arts.com

32. Timothy Carless MSGD
www.timothygardendesign.co.uk

33. Barry Chambers MSGD
www.changingscenes.co.uk

34. Ruth Chivers FSGD
Visit the SGD website for
contact details

35. Marie Clarke MSGD
www.clarkeassociates.cc

36. Mhairi Clutson MSGD
www.grozone.co.uk

37. Rosemary Coldstream MSGD
www.rosemarycoldstream.com

38. Douglas Coltart MSGD
www.viridarium.co.uk

39. Sally Court FSGD
www.cgd-landscape-design.com

40. Paul Cowell MSGD
www.pclandscapes.co.uk

41. Josie Cox MSGD
www.wilkinsoncox.com

42. Stuart Craine MSGD
www.stuartcraine.com

43. Cheryl Cummings MSGD
www.gardendesignerwales.co.uk

44. John Davies FSGD
www.johnadavieslandscapes.com

45. Caroline Davy MSGD
www.carolinedavy.co.uk

46. Chris Deakin MSGD
www.deakinlock.co.uk

47. Tommaso del Buono MSGD
delbuono-gazerwitz.co.uk

48. Susan Dodge MSGD
www.susandodge.co.uk

49. Alison Dove MSGD
www.dovegardendesign.com

50. Annabel Downs FSGD
annabeldowns.co.uk

51. Paul Dracott MSGD
www.pdgd.co.uk

52. Andrew Duff MSGD
www.andrewduffgardendesign.com

53. Ann Dukes MSGD
www.paceybuckgardendesign.co.uk

54. Jacqueline Easton MSGD
www.jacqueline-easton.co.uk

55. Sarah Eberle MSGD
www.saraheberle.com

56. Liz Elfick-Wood MSGD
www.allseasonslandscape.co.uk

57. Helen Elks-Smith MSGD
www.elks-smith.co.uk

58. Peter Eustance MSGD
www.symphonicgardens.com

59. Chris Eves MSGD
www.evesandlewis.co.uk

60. Moira Farnham MSGD
www.moirafarnham.co.uk

61. Vanessa Faulkner MSGD
www.colebyandfaulkner.co.uk

62. Mark Fenton MSGD
www.markfentondesigns.co.uk

63. Jill Fenwick MSGD
www.jillfenwick.co.uk

64. Andrew Fisher Tomlin FSGD
www.fishertomlin.com

65. Kristina Fitzsimmons MSGD
www.kristinafitzsimmons.co.uk

66. Julia Fogg MSGD
www.juliafogg.com

67. Jane Follis MSGD
www.janefollis.com

68. Jonathan Ford MSGD
www.fordlandscape.co.uk

69. Tracy Foster MSGD
www.tracyfostergardendesign.co.uk

70. Patricia Fox MSGD
www.aralia.org.uk

71. Robert Frier MSGD
www.charlesworthdesign.com

72. Paul Gazerwitz MSGD
delbuono-gazerwitz.co.uk

73. Gill German MSGD
www.beescapes.co.uk

74. Luciano Giubbilei MSGD
www.lucianogiubbilei.com

75. **Belinda Goldsmith MSGD**
belinda-goldsmith.co.uk

76. **Alasdair Gordon-Hall MSGD**
www.gardenscenejersey.net

77. **Gordon Gray MSGD**
www.planscapes.net

78. **Marcus Green MSGD**
www.
marcusgreenhorticulturaldesign.
co.uk

79. **Roderick Griffin FSGD**
www.roderickgriffin-landscape.
com

80. **Chris Gutteridge MSGD**
www.secondnaturegardens.co.uk

81. **Sarah Hammond MSGD**
www.sarahhammonddesign.com

82. **Fiona Harrison MSGD**
www.fhgd.com

83. **Anthea Harrison MSGD**
www.antheaharrison.co.uk

84. **Louise Harrison-Holland MSGD**
www.bluetulipgardendesign.
co.uk

85. **Catherine Heatherington MSGD**
www.chdesigns.co.uk

86. **Paul Hensey MSGD**
www.paulhensey.com

87. **Joanna Herald MSGD**
www.joannaherald.com

88. **Thomas Hoblyn MSGD**
www.thomashoblyn.com

89. **Fiona Hopes FSGD**
www.song-of-the-earth.com

90. **Lucy Huntington FSGD**
www.lucyhuntington.co.uk

91. **Jane Inge MSGD**
www.agardendesigner.co.nz

92. **Dawn Isaac MSGD**
www.dawn-isaac.com

93. **Spike Jackson MSGD**
www.sjdesign.co.uk

94. **Pamela Johnson MSGD**
www.pamelajohnson.co.uk

95. **Alex Johnson MSGD**
www.elemental-landscape-
architects.co.uk

96. **Julia Jones MSGD**
www.juliajonesgardendesign.com

97. **David Keary MSGD**
www.keary-coles-design.co.uk

98. **Anne Keenan MSGD**
www.annekeenan.co.uk

99. **Barry Kellington MSGD**
www.honleygardendesign.co.uk

100. **John Kenny MSGD**
www.kennydesign.co.uk

101. **Richard Key FSGD**
www.richardkey.co.uk

102. **Ian Kitson FSGD**
www.iankitson.com

103. **Cheri La May MSGD**
www.earthworksnorth.co.uk

104. **Rose Lennard MSGD**
www.chameleongardens.co.uk

105. **Arabella Lennox-Boyd MSGD**
www.arabellalennoxboyd.com

106. **Dan Lobb MSGD**
www.daniellobb.co.uk

107. **Jason Lock MSGD**
www.deakinlock.co.uk

108. **Paul Luker MSGD**
www.paulluker.com

109. **Tim Lynch MSGD**
www.tlassociates.co.uk

110. **Sally Marlow MSGD**
www.marlowconsulting.co.uk

111. **Andrew Marson MSGD**
www.bespokegardens.co.uk

112. **Sarah Massey FSGD**
www.sarahmassey.co.uk

113. **Laurence Maunder MSGD**
www.laurencemaunder.co.uk

114. **Caroline May MSGD**
www.carolinemaydesign.co.uk

115. **Emma Mazzullo MSGD**
www.alblandscapeassociates.
com

116. **Sam McGowan MSGD**
www.sam-mcgowan.co.uk

117. **Merilen Mentaal MSGD**
www.mentaallandscapes.com

118. **Jacquetta Menzies MSGD**
www.jacquettamenzies.co.uk

119. **Cherry Mills MSGD**
www.cmgardendesign.com

120. **Jane Mooney MSGD**
www.janemooney.co.uk

121. **Sarah Morgan MSGD**
www.sarahmorgangardens.co.uk

122. **Karolyn Mowll MSGD**
www.turningleafgd.co.uk

123. **Kevin Murphy MSGD**
www.kevinmurphy.co.uk

124. **Robert Myers MSGD**
www.robertmyers-associates.
co.uk

125. **John Nash MSGD**
www.johnnashassociates.co.uk

126. **Andrea Newill MSGD**
www.andreanewillgardendesign.
co.uk

127. Matthew Nichol MSGD
www.mngardendesign.co.uk

128. Philippa O'Brien MSGD
www.pipobriengardendesign.com

129. Alexander Oesterheld MSGD
www.die-gartenidee.de

130. Karen O'Keeffe MSGD
www.manchestergardendesign.co.uk

131. Andrea Parsons MSGD
www.theparsonsgarden.co.uk

132. Christine Parsons MSGD
www.hallamgardendesign.co.uk

133. Ali Paterson MSGD
www.alipaterson.com

134. Trisha Patterson MSGD
www.trishapatterson.co.uk

135. Janine Pattison MSGD
www.janinepattison.com

136. Amanda Patton MSGD
www.amandapatton.co.uk

137. Anthony Paul FSGD
www.anthonypaullandscapedesign.com

138. Dan Pearson MSGD
www.danpearsonstudio.com

139. Jane Peterson MSGD
www.janepetersongardendesign.co.uk

140. Nigel Philips FSGD
www.nigelphilips.co.uk

141. Emma Plunket MSGD
www.plunketgardens.com

142. Keith Pocock MSGD
www.stephenwoodhams.com

143. Jonathan Pringle MSGD
Visit the SGD website for contact details

144. Chris Prior MSGD
www.chrispriordesign.co.uk

145. Mark Pumphrey MSGD
www.external-designs.co.uk

146. Paul Richards MSGD
www.paulrichardsgardendesign.co.uk

147. Jilayne Rickards MSGD
www.jilaynerickards.com

148. Debbie Roberts MSGD
www.acreswild.co.uk

149. David Robinson MSGD
www.upthegardenpath.net

150. Richard Romang MSGD
www.richardromang.co.uk

151. Katherine Roper MSGD
www.katherineroper.co.uk

152. Sara Jane Rothwell MSGD
www.londongardendesigner.com

153. Charlotte Rowe MSGD
www.charlotterowe.com

154. Charles Rutherfoord MSGD
www.charlesrutherfoord.net

155. Elaine Rutherford MSGD
www.topiagardendesign.co.uk

156. Ana Sanchez-Martin MSGD
www.germinatedesign.com

157. Juliet Sargeant MSGD
www.julietdesigns.co.uk

158. James Scott MSGD
www.thegardenco.co.uk

159. James Seymour FSGD
www.seymours-landscapes.com

160. David Sisley FSGD
www.gardendesignsandlandscapes.co.uk

161. Ian Smith MSGD
www.acreswild.co.uk

162. Lucy Sommers MSGD
www.lucysommersgardens.com

163. Fiona Stephenson MSGD
www.fionastephensondesigns.com

164. David Stevens FSGD
www.david-stevens.co.uk

165. Tom Stuart-Smith MSGD
www.tomstuartsmith.co.uk

166. Andy Sturgeon FSGD
www.andysturgeon.com

167. Joe Swift MSGD
www.modulargarden.com

168. Sue Tallents MSGD
www.suetallentsgardens.co.uk

169. Helen Taylor MSGD
www.helentaylorgardendesign.co.uk

170. Kathy Taylor MSGD
www.kathytaylordesigns.co.uk

171. Robin Templar Williams FSGD
www.robinwilliams.co.uk

172. Gillian Temple MSGD
www.gilliantemple.co.uk

173. Catherine Thomas MSGD
www.catherinethomas.co.uk

174. Kate Thornton MSGD
www.gardenvisions.co.uk

175. Sally Tierney MSGD
www.yorkshiregardendesigner.co.uk

176. Julie Toll FSGD
www.julietoll.co.uk

177. Sue Townsend MSGD
www.suetownsendgardendesign.co.uk

178. Chevrel Traher MSGD
www.englishgardens.com.tr

179. Lizzie Tulip MSGD
www.lizzietulip.com

180. Gianna Utilini MSGD
www.giannautilini.co.uk

181. Tina Vallis MSGD
www.tinavallis.co.uk

182. Julie Vann MSGD
www.outerspacesgardendesign.com

183. Malcolm Veitch FSGD
www.veitchgardendesign.co.uk

184. Louis Vincent MSGD
www.louisvincent.co.uk

185. Helen Voisey MSGD
www.helenvoisey.co.uk

186. Michelle Wake MSGD
www.greenwavedesign.co.uk

187. Jan Walker MSGD
Visit the SGD website for contact details

188. Steven Warren-Brown MSGD
www.ygslandscapes.co.uk

189. Roger Webster MSGD
www.webstergardens.co.uk

190. Andrew Wenham MSGD
www.andrew-wenham.co.uk

191. Cleve West MSGD
www.clevewest.com

192. Christine Whatley MSGD
www.sylvanstudio.co.uk

193. Rob Whitehead MSGD
www.pickardschool.com

194. Carol Whitehead MSGD
www.carolwhitehead.co.uk

195. Geoffrey Whiten FSGD
Visit the SGD website for contact details

196. Jano Williams MSGD
www.janowilliams.com

197. Robin Williams FSGD
www.robinwilliams.co.uk

198. Andrew Wilson FSGD
www.wmstudio.co.uk

199. John Wyer FSGD
www.bowleswyer.co.uk

200. Chris Zbrożyna MSGD
www.paperbark.co.uk

The following designers also work outside the UK. Others may also work in other countries; contact individual designers to discuss specific projects.

Marie-Louise Agius MSGD

James Basson MSGD

Sarah Bicknell MSGD

Dan Bowyer MSGD

Denise Cadwallader FSGD

Timothy Carless MSGD

Douglas Coltart MSGD

Sally Court FSGD

Stuart Craine MSGD

John Davies FSGD

Alison Dove MSGD

Andrew Fisher Tomlin FSGD

Patricia Fox MSGD

Gill German MSGD

Lucy Huntington FSGD

Jane Inge MSGD

Arabella Lennox-Boyd MSGD

Jason Lock MSGD

Merilen Mentaal MSGD

Philippa O'Brien MSGD

Alexander Oesterheld MSGD

Anthony Paul MSGD

Dan Pearson MSGD

Debbie Roberts MSGD

Charlotte Rowe MSGD

Ian Smith MSGD

Fiona Stephenson MSGD

David Stevens FSGD

Andy Sturgeon FSGD

Tom Stuart-Smith MSGD

Robin Williams FSGD

Julie Toll FSGD

Chevrel Traher MSGD

Cleve West MSGD

Andrew Wilson FSGD

John Wyer FSGD

Index of SGD designers

A

Acres Wild 40, 43, 49, 56–7, 64, 66, 69, 70, 73, 87, 92, 94, 97, 98, 100, 109, 110, 116, 124, 132, 135, 143
Adcock, Sue 49, 61, 92, 158
Alder, Fern 147
Alexander, Rosemary 106

B

Basson, James 63, 98, 120–1, 134, 135
Brookes, John 7, 69, 113, 174
Buckland, Mandy 26, 63, 65, 78, 80, 119
Burns, Andrew 153
Butler, Sean 134

C

Cadwallader, Denise 55, 84, 104, 114, 130, 131
Coldstream, Rosemary 55
Coltart, Douglas 75
Craine, Stuart 26, 29, 47, 112
Cummings, Cheryl 86, 148

D

Davy, Caroline 106
Deakin, Chris (DeakinLock) 129
del Buono, Tommaso 16

E

Eberle, Sarah 55, 153
Elks-Smith, Helen 40, 96, 98, 118

F

Fenwick, Jill 97
Fisher Tomlin, Andrew 2–3, 14, 81, 83, 85, 112, 124, 141, 162–3
Fogg, Julia 101, 117, 154
Foster, Tracey 148
Fox, Patricia 65, 68, 103, 112, 127, 138–9

G

Gazerwitz, Paul 16
Gibson, John 53–4
Giubbilei, Luciano 22–3
Gutteridge, Chris 123, 140, 141

H

Harrison-Holland, Louise 66, 94, 136
Heatherington, Catherine 94, 114
Hensey, Paul 63, 65, 143, 144
Herald, Joanna 154
Hoblyn, Thomas 34, 40, 110

K

Keenan, Anne 70, 73
Kitson, Ian 10–11, 40, 72, 87, 109, 116, 141, 153

L

Lennox-Boyd, Arabella 36–7, 43, 70, 72, 76, 110, 114
Lock, Jason (DeakinLock) 15, 76, 143

M

Massey, Sarah 87
Mentaal, Merilen 29, 114, 117, 129
Mills, Cherry 26

N

Nash, John 83, 126, 127

P

Parsons, Chris 154
Pattison, Janine 81, 118, 136, 27
Patton, Amanda 86, 97, 100, 122, 123, 129
Paul, Anthony 61, 69, 76, 77, 104
Pearson, Dan 13, 44–5, 114, 154
Philips, Nigel 73, 84, 104, 106

R

Roberts, Debbie *see Acres Wild*
Rothwell, Sara Jane 15, 29, 63, 75
Rowe, Charlotte 14, 21, 25, 58–59, 62, 63, 66, 80, 82, 91, 106
Rutherfoord, Charles 34, 91

S

Sanchez-Martin, Ana 71, 126
Scape Design 134
Scott, James 72, 85, 89, 92, 93, 109, 114, 117
Smith, Ian *see Acres Wild*
Sommers, Lucy 52, 101, 131
Stephenson, Fiona 94, 109, 149
Stevens, David 33
Stuart-Smith, Tom 13, 20, 35, 38, 103, 105, 156–7
Sturgeon, Andy 20, 29, 30–1, 42, 64, 66, 76, 82, 136
Swift, Joe 49

T

Toll, Julie 50–1, 75
Townsend, Sue 91, 92, 99, 102

V

Vallis, Tina 81, 136

W

Webster, Roger 89, 97
West, Cleve 49, 68, 81, 85, 91, 98, 102, 113, 153, 154
Wilson, Andrew (Wilson McWilliam) 9, 43, 94, 105, 110, 124, 136, 153
Wyer, John 78, 84, 124, 152, 153

Z

Zbrożyna, Chris 1, 76, 117

Index

Page numbers in **bold** indicate a subject discussed in a coloured panel or box. Plant styles and planting groups are indexed, but planting up particular gardens and areas are grouped under *planting*.

Photographic acknowledgements

t = top; b = bottom; l = left; r = right; m = middle

Acres Wild: 57br, 4tr, 41r, 42r, 48tr, 56–57, 64mr, 66b, 68bl, 71bm, 73mr, 75bl, 86bl, 92br, 94tr, 97mr, 98tr, 100–101tm, 108–109bm, 110tl, 116tl, 132, 135b, 142tl

Sue Adcock: 48tl, 60, 92bl, 159

Laura Antebi: 78bl

James Basson: 5bl, 120–121, 135tl, 63tm, 98br

Mark Bolton/Homes & Gardens/IPC+ Syndication: 19

Sean Butler: 134

Denise Cadwallader: 55br, 84–85tm, 104bl, 114tr, 131mr

Cityscapes/www.cityscapes.org.uk: 152b

Douglas Coltart: 75br

Stuart Craine: 112tl

Cheryl Cummings: 86tl, 148bl

Caroline Davy: 106mr

Dr Nigel Dunnett: 146bl

Helen Elks-Smith: 40t, 97ml, 98bl, 118tr

Jill Fenwick: 97t

Helen Fickling: 21t, 42l, 64tr, 76tm, 82t

Andrew Fisher Tomlin: 2–3, 14t, 80bl, 83br, 85br, 112–113tm, 162–163

Julia Fogg: 101tr, 116–117bm, 155bl

Patricia Fox: 65tl, 68tl, 74mr, 102tr, 112br, 127t, 138–139

GAP: 135tr, 142bm, 160

Garden Company: 72tr, 89, 109br, 116bm, 85mr

Gloster Furniture/gloster.com: 122

Steve Gorton: 100br

Great Little Trading Company/gltc.co.uk: 133tl

greencube garden and landscape design: 26tr, 63ml, 65ml, 74bl, 79, 80tl, 119br, 125bl

Chris Gutteridge: 123mr, 140b

Harpur Garden Picture Library: 30–31, 33, 78mr/Design by Jo Thompson

Louise Harrison-Holland: 5tr, 67b, 94m, 137tr

Catherine Heatherington: 94bl, 114bl

Paul Hensey: 63br, 65bl, 143

Jackie Herald: 154l

Ian Hodgson: 146br

Thomas Hoblyn: 40b

Jason Ingram: 70–71t

Anne Keenan: 70–71bm, 73bm, 74br

Ian Kitson: 51br, 41l, 50–51, 72–73tm, 74ml, 108–109tr, 140t, 161

Arabella Lennox-Boyd: 37r, 43b

DeakinLock: 15t, 76m, 142bl

Marianne Majerus: 7t, 7b, 10–11, 12, 14b, 15b, 16, 20, 25, 26tl, 28t, 29b, 34ml, 35, 38, 47, 49l, 49r, 54, 62–63 l, 75mr, 75tr, 80–81tm, 83tr, 86br, 104–105br, 106br, 106–107tm, 110br, 116–117tm, 126t, 130, 144/Design by Lynne Marcus, 156–157

Sarah Massey: 87

Wilson McWilliam: 8, 18tr, 43t, 94–95m, 125br, 136bl, 153tl

Merilen Mentaal: 29t, 114bm, 116bl, 129

Cherry Mills: 26bl

Box topiary and edging lends a formal note to this richly planted suburban garden.

DESIGN BY JOHN BROOKES

Alex Moira: 94br, 108tm, 149t

John Nash: 82–83bm, 127b

Clive Nichols: 126b

Charlotte Noar: 64tl, 69tr, 100tl

Brian North: 123tl/ Sofa by Garden Furniture Centre/ gardenfurniturecentre.co.uk, 128tl, 131tr/Design by Amanda Waring and Laura Arison, 133tr, 133br/Design by Claire Broadbent, 141mr, 142br/Design by Jenni Cairns and Sophie Antonelli, 145m/Design by Jennifer Hirsch, 147tl/Design by Kate Frey, 147bl/Design by Design by Jenni Cairns and Sophie Antonelli, 147br/ Design by Heidi Harvey and Fern Adler, 148br, 151br/ Design by Hugo Bugg, 147tl

Chris Parsons: 154r

Janine Pattison: 27, 80bm, 118tl, 136mr

Amanda Patton: 5tl, 86tr, 97br, 123tr, 128tr

Dan Pearson: 13, 44–45

Nigel Philips: 4br, 18bl, 73br, 84br, 104tl, 107bl

Alan Pollok-Morris: 31r, 72–73bl, 76bm, 110tr, 114br, 45r, 34br, 68bm, 110bl

Ana Sanchez-Martin: 71br

Sara Jane Rothwell: 63mr

Charlotte Rowe: 4ml, 21b, 58–59, 66t, 91tm

Charles Rutherfoord: 34bl, 91ml

James Scott: 92ml, 114mr

Jane Sebire: 36–37, 93

Shutterstock: 91br, 92tr, 99l, 103, 107tr, 111, 115, 119tl, 131bl, 141bl, 145br, 149b, 150bl, 150br, 151bl, 151m, 153m

Lucy Smith: 78tr

Lucy Sommers: 52, 101bl

Nicola Stocken: 55tl

Derek St Romaine: 68–69 tm, 81tm, 85bl, 90–91m, 98tl, 102bl, 113tl, 155br

Andy Sturgeon: 155tr

Jo Thompson: 124tr

Sue Townsend: 91mr, 92mr, 99r, 102tl

Tina Vallis: 5br, 80–81br, 137tl

Vertigarden/www.vertigarden.co.uk: 145bl, 145bm

Roger Webster: 74m, 88, 97bl

Cleve West: 153b

Andrew Wilson: 104–105tr

Steve Wooster: 22–23, 28b, 61, 67t, 68–69br, 69tr, 76bl, 102br, 104tm, 113mr, 114ml, 124tl, 141tr, 153tr, 155ml, 174

John Wyer: 78br, 84tl, 125tr, 152t

Chris Zbrozyna: 1, 76–77r, 117tm

Author's acknowledgements

I would sincerely like to thank all the members of the Society of Garden Designers and others who provided inspirational examples of their work, including the majority of the photographs and illustrations used in this book. Without them all this would not have been possible.

I would also like to thank Helen Griffin at Frances Lincoln who commissioned me to undertake the project, the editor Zia Allaway for keeping things on track, and Becky Clarke for her inspired design. Finally, I would like to thank my parents for first fostering my interest in horticulture and my wife Judith, whose patience and support while I worked on the book over many months knew no bounds.